Witness Lee

The Work of the Holy Spirit

Living Stream Ministry
Anaheim, California

First Edition, August 1999.

ISBN 0-7363-0663-3

Published by

Living Stream Ministry
2431 W. La Palma Ave., Anaheim, CA 92801 U.S.A.
P. O. Box 2121, Anaheim, CA 92814 U.S.A.

Printed in the United States of America

99 00 01 02 03 04 / 9 8 7 6 5 4 3 2 1

CONTENTS

PREFACE

This book is composed of messages given by Brother Witness Lee in a training in Altadena, California in the summer of 1963. These messages were not reviewed by the speaker.

CHAPTER ONE

THE TWO ASPECTS OF THE WORK
OF THE SPIRIT

Scripture Reading: John 7:37-39; Luke 24:49; Acts 1:5, 8; John 20:22; 14:16-17; Rom. 8:2; Eph. 1:13-14; 4:30; 1 John 2:20, 27, 1; John 14:26; 15:26; 16:7

The work of the Holy Spirit is a great and deep subject. In these messages we cannot go into detail on this subject, but we will cover some main points.

THE SPIRIT BEING THE DIVINE TRANSMISSION
OF THE TRIUNE GOD

As we know, God is one God in three persons. Therefore, we call Him the Triune God. This does not mean that there are three Gods, but rather one God in three persons—the Father, the Son, and the Spirit. The Father is the source, the Son is the expression, and the Spirit is the communion, the divine transmission. The Father is the source in eternity, in a realm to which we cannot go and which we cannot touch (1 Tim. 6:16). The Son is the expression of the Father. He is the Word of God, the expression of the invisible God. However, we still need another Person, the Spirit, so that all that God is as the Father and is expressed in the Son might be transmitted, communicated, to us. Therefore, the Spirit is the transmission, the communion, of what the Father is and what the Son of God expresses.

We may illustrate the Triune God in His divine economy with water in three stages. The first stage is the water in the source, the fountain, and the second stage is the water in the spring. The water comes out of the fountain as the source, and the spring contains the water. The third stage is the flow, the current to flow out the water, to bring the water to all places, to reach other places with the water. These are not three different waters, but one water in three stages—the water at the source, the water in the spring, and the water in the current. God the Father is the source; Christ, who is God the Son, is the divine well, the divine spring; and the Holy Spirit is the divine flow, the divine current to reach us.

It is as the Holy Spirit that God in Christ can visit us and reach us. In Himself, God the Father cannot reach us, and even when expressed in God the Son, He still cannot reach us today. It is as the Spirit and by the Spirit that God the Father in God the Son can reach us, visit us, come upon us, and come into us. Therefore, in the divine economy, the Spirit is the third and last stage in which God comes out to visit us.

THE TWO ASPECTS OF THE WORK OF THE SPIRIT

According to the teachings of the Scriptures, the work of the Holy Spirit is in two aspects. If we are not clear about the two aspects of the work of the Holy Spirit, we cannot properly know the truth concerning the Spirit. Several verses speak clearly concerning these two aspects. John 7:37-39 says, "Now on the last day, the great day of the feast, Jesus stood and cried out, saying, If anyone thirsts, let him come to Me and drink. He who believes into Me, as the Scripture said, out of his innermost being shall flow rivers of living water. But this He said concerning the Spirit, whom those who believed into Him were about to receive; for the Spirit was not yet, because Jesus had not yet been glorified." In this passage, there are two main points to remember. First, the Spirit, whom the disciples were about to receive, would be in them and would flow out from within them. Second, the Holy Spirit here is likened to water for drinking. Anyone who thirsts can come to the Lord and drink of this living water, who is the Holy Spirit. In addition, John 14:17 says, "Even the Spirit of reality, whom the world cannot receive, because it does not behold Him or know Him; but you know Him, because He abides with you and shall be in you." These verses clearly say that the Spirit is the living water to drink, and He is within us. This is one aspect of the Holy Spirit.

Luke 24:49 shows us the other aspect of the Holy Spirit. It says, "And behold, I send forth the promise of My Father upon you; but as for you, stay in the city until you put on power from on high." The promise of the Father is the Holy Spirit. Please notice the word *upon;* it is different from *in.* We all know the difference between *upon* and *in.* In this verse, the Holy Spirit comes upon us, not into us. To put on power is to be clothed with power. In the Gospel of John the Holy Spirit is likened to living water to drink, but in the Gospel of Luke the Holy Spirit is likened to clothing upon us. Water is different from clothing. When we drink water, it is within us, and when we put on clothing, it is upon us. The Spirit upon us as clothing is the power from on high, while the Spirit within us as the water we drink is for life. On the one hand, we have the Spirit within us as life, and on the other hand, we have the Spirit upon us as power. The Spirit within us as life is likened to water for drinking, and the Spirit upon us as power is likened to clothing.

In the Old Testament, when Elijah was taken up into the heavens, he left his outer garment, his mantle, to Elisha (2 Kings 2:9-15). In that way Elisha received the power which Elijah had. The mantle is an item of clothing, signifying that Elisha was clothed with power from on high. The Lord ascended to the heavens as Elijah did, and He sent His Spirit as clothing down from the heavens. Now we are clothed with this power. On the one hand, the Holy Spirit is within us as the water we drink, and on the other hand, the Holy Spirit is upon us as our clothing. These are two different aspects.

Luke also wrote the book of Acts. Acts 1:5 says, "For John baptized with water, but you shall be baptized in the Holy Spirit not many days from now." Verse 8 continues, "But you shall receive power when the Holy Spirit comes upon you." Verse 5 says the disciples would be baptized in, not merely with, the Holy Spirit. When we are baptized in water, we are put into the water, and the water is upon us. In the same way, we have been baptized in the Holy Spirit, and the Holy Spirit is upon us. This is the power in verse 8. This baptism was accomplished on the day of Pentecost. On the day of

Pentecost, the Holy Spirit came down from heaven upon the disciples, and they were baptized in the Holy Spirit.

THE APPLICATION OF THE TWO ASPECTS OF THE WORK OF THE SPIRIT

With the Lord Jesus

We may now apply the principle of the two aspects of the work of the Holy Spirit. First, we can see the work of the Holy Spirit with the Lord Jesus. Both Matthew and Luke tell us that the Lord Jesus was born of the Holy Spirit (Matt. 1:18, 20; Luke 1:35). Before He came out to work for God at the age of thirty, He was already filled with the Holy Spirit. However, it was at the time of His baptism in water that the heavens opened, and the Holy Spirit came upon Him as a dove (Matt. 3:16). This does not mean that before the Holy Spirit came upon Him, He did not have the Holy Spirit. Because He was born of the Holy Spirit, the Holy Spirit had been in Him and filled Him for thirty years. However, at the age of thirty, when He came out to work for God to preach the gospel, He needed to be baptized on the one hand, in the water, and on the other hand, in the Holy Spirit. The Holy Spirit needed to come upon Him as power so that He could preach the gospel. These two aspects are very clear.

With the Disciples

We may also apply these two aspects to the first group of disciples, including Peter and John. When did those disciples receive the Holy Spirit? When I was young, I was taught by certain books and teachers that those disciples received the Holy Spirit on the day of Pentecost. In actuality, the disciples received the Holy Spirit on the day of the Lord's resurrection. On the evening of the day in which the Lord was resurrected, He came to His disciples. John 20:22 says, "And when He had said this, He breathed into them and said to them, Receive the Holy Spirit."

In chapters fourteen and sixteen, when the Lord was about to die, He promised the disciples that after His death and resurrection He would send the Spirit of reality to them.

Verses 16-17 of chapter fourteen say, "And I will ask the Father, and He will give you another Comforter, that He may be with you forever, even the Spirit of reality, whom the world cannot receive, because it does not behold Him or know Him; but you know Him, because He abides with you and shall be in you." This promise concerning the coming of the Holy Spirit in chapters fourteen and sixteen was not fulfilled on the day of Pentecost but in the evening of the day of resurrection, in chapter twenty, when the Lord came to them with the Spirit, breathed into them, and said, "Receive the Holy Spirit." This was the Holy Spirit of life, the Spirit who came into the disciples as life. This is the first aspect of the work of the Spirit.

The first promise concerning the Spirit was that the Lord Himself would ask the Father to send another Comforter, the Spirit of reality. This promise was fulfilled on the day of resurrection. Forty days after the resurrection, when the Lord was about to ascend to the heavens, He promised the disciples again, telling them to stay in Jerusalem until He sent the promise of the Father, the Holy Spirit of power, from on high. This was another promise concerning the Holy Spirit. This second promise, concerning not the Spirit of life but the Spirit of power, was fulfilled on the day of Pentecost.

Before the day of Pentecost, the disciples already had the Spirit of reality. The day of Pentecost is in Acts 2. Before that time, the one hundred twenty disciples prayed together for ten days in one accord, and they understood how to expound the Psalms (Acts 1:14, 20). We may compare this to the prior situation of the disciples. When the Lord was going to the cross, the disciples quarreled with one another about who would be the greatest. This was because at that time they did not have the Holy Spirit within them. It was on the day of resurrection when the Lord came to them and breathed on them that they received the Spirit of reality and life. Because of this, they were able to stay together and pray with one accord before the day of Pentecost.

Moreover, they prayed in the spirit. Without the Spirit dwelling in them they could not have done this. They gave up their country, their home in Galilee, and they stayed in

Jerusalem under the threatenings of the people. At that time in Jerusalem the people were threatening them, but they had the boldness to stay there and pray in one accord for ten days. How could they have done this without the help of the Holy Spirit dwelling within them? It would have been impossible. However, they had the Spirit of life, the Spirit of reality, within them already. Therefore, they could do these things. This is a strong proof that before the day of Pentecost, the disciples already had the Holy Spirit of reality and of life.

They had the Holy Spirit of life within, but they had not received the Holy Spirit of power without. It was on the day of Pentecost, as they were praying together in the upper room, that the Holy Spirit of power came down from heaven upon them, and the Lord Jesus as the Head of the Body baptized them as the Body. On that day the Lord was the Baptizer, and the one hundred twenty were the representatives of the Body. The Head baptized the Body in the Holy Spirit.

To drink water is to take water into us, but to be baptized in water is not to drink it; it is to get into the water. On the one hand, the water is in us, and on the other hand, the water is upon us. Resurrection is a matter of life. On that day of life, the day of resurrection, the disciples received the Holy Spirit as the Spirit of life. The day of Pentecost, however, was a day for the work of the preaching of the gospel. Therefore, the disciples needed power, so the Holy Spirit came down as power upon them. These are two aspects. One is the inward aspect, and the other is the outward aspect. One is the aspect of life, and the other is the aspect of power.

SIX ITEMS OF THE SPIRIT WITHIN US

Now we must see what the Spirit is to us when He comes into us. As we have seen, He is the Spirit of life to be life to us (Rom. 8:2). Second, He is the Spirit of reality (John 14:17). He is within us as the reality. Reality is not merely doctrine. The Spirit is the reality of all that God and Christ are. God is love, but without the Spirit of reality within us we do not have the reality of love. If we have the Spirit of reality within us, we have the reality of love. God is also light, but if we do not have the Spirit of reality, we do not have the reality of light. All that God and Christ are is in the Holy Spirit as the divine reality to us.

Third, the Holy Spirit within us is a seal (Eph. 1:13; 4:30). When we believe in the Lord Jesus as our Savior, we belong to God, and God puts a seal upon us. When I buy a new book, I put my seal on it. This means that the book is mine. When we believe in the Lord Jesus, we become God's. We belong to God, so God puts His seal upon us, or within us. This seal is the Holy Spirit. Moreover, to put a seal on something we possess makes that thing exactly the same as the seal. The seal of the Holy Spirit within us is an element within us that is exactly the same as God.

Fourth, Ephesians 1:14 says that the Spirit is also a pledge. A pledge is a down payment. The Holy Spirit is the pledge, the guarantee, that all that God is and all that God has is our portion. The Spirit as the seal within us testifies that we belong to God, and the Spirit as the pledge within us is a guarantee that God belongs to us, that all that God is and all that God has are our portion. We may say, "O Father, You must give me all that You have and all that You are, because I have the Spirit as the guarantee."

Fifth, the Spirit is the anointing (1 John 2:20, 27). We have the Spirit within us who is always anointing us. While He is anointing us, He also is bothering us.

Sixth, the Spirit is the Comforter (John 14:16, 26; 15:26; 16:7). The Greek word for *Comforter* is *Paraclete*. In 1 John 2:1, this word is translated as *Advocate*. The Paraclete has a daily application and a legal application. In daily life, the Paraclete is always with us to serve us and care for us. In the legal sense, the paraclete is an attorney, a lawyer in a court of law who pleads for us. In our daily life, the Holy Spirit always accompanies us to care for us and to meet all our daily needs. Concerning the righteous law of God, however, Jesus Christ as the Advocate is the attorney in the heavenly court always pleading for us.

The Holy Spirit as life, reality, the seal, the pledge, and the anointing is everything to us, and as the Comforter He takes care of us in our daily life. However, if something happens to us in the heavenly court, the Advocate is our attorney to defend us and plead for us. These are the aspects of the Holy Spirit within us.

CHAPTER TWO

THE INWARD AND OUTWARD FILLING
OF THE HOLY SPIRIT

Scripture Reading: 1 Cor. 12:13; Acts 2:2, 4; 13:52; Eph. 5:18;
Luke 1:15, 41, 67; Acts 4:8, 31; 9:17; 13:9; Luke 4:1; Acts
6:3, 5; 7:55; 11:24; 8:15-17; 10:44-47; 19:2, 6; Eph. 1:13-14;
Acts 1:5; 11:15-17

TWO ASPECTS OF THE HOLY SPIRIT

As we saw in the previous chapter, the work of the Holy
Spirit is of two aspects: the inward aspect and the outward
aspect. The Holy Spirit comes into us and comes upon us. The
Holy Spirit in us is for life and as life, and the Holy Spirit
upon us is for power and as power. As proper, normal Christians, we need life and power. Life is for the Christian walk
and living, and power is for the Christian work and service.
For our daily walk and living as the Lord's children we need
the inner life. For the work, the gospel preaching, the winning
of souls, the service, and the ministry we need power. Therefore, throughout the entire Scriptures the Holy Spirit is
revealed to us in these two aspects. One aspect is that the
Holy Spirit comes into us and dwells in us to be life to us, the
flow of life, the life supply, and all matters related to life. The
other aspect is that the Holy Spirit comes upon us as power to
empower us, to endow us with power, that we may be powerful and prevailing in the Lord's service.

The Spirit of Life as Breath

In the previous message we saw several items of the Holy
Spirit within us. He is the Spirit of life, the Spirit of reality,
the seal, the pledge, the anointing, and the Comforter. After

the Lord died, He came back to the disciples on the day of His resurrection. When He came back to the disciples, He brought the Spirit of life to them. He breathed into them and said, "Receive the Holy Spirit" (John 20:22). The Spirit was breath breathed by the Lord. We all know that breath is not for power; breath is for life.

The Spirit of Power for Preaching

After His ascension, however, on the day of Pentecost, the Lord poured down the Holy Spirit from heaven upon the disciples as power. This pouring down was like a heavy rain. In this way all the disciples were empowered. Before the day of Pentecost, the disciples were together for ten days. Those were not days of power but days of life. For the one hundred twenty to be in one accord and pray was a matter of life, not of power. But on the day of Pentecost, when the Spirit came down upon them, they stood up to speak to the people, and three thousand people were brought under conviction. This was a matter of power; the disciples had power in their preaching. Therefore, to have the Spirit of life within us is one thing, while to have the Spirit of power without is another.

The Spirit in the Gospels of John and Luke

As we have seen, the Gospel of John deals with the matters of life. In this Gospel the Spirit of life is likened to living water for us to drink. According to the Gospel of Luke, however, the Spirit of power is likened to clothing that we put on, because this Gospel deals with the gospel of forgiveness, which requires power for preaching to bring people under conviction. To drink water is one thing, while to put on an item of clothing is another thing. We cannot say that these two are the same. In my own room I can drink water without proper clothing, but when I come out to minister, I must put on proper clothes. If I do not have proper clothing covering me, I am not qualified or equipped to come out to minister. On the other hand I may be dressed very well, but I may still be thirsty because I have not drunk anything. This illustrates the two aspects of the Holy Spirit. The Spirit of life within us is to refresh us, satisfy us, and quench our thirst. This is one aspect. But to have the Holy Spirit as power to equip us, to empower us, is another aspect. We should not consider these two aspects as one. Many think that the work of the Holy Spirit has only one aspect. This is a problem among the Lord's children today.

The Spirit Within for Regeneration, Indwelling, and Infilling

Concerning the Holy Spirit within us, there are several steps. The first step is that the Spirit comes into us to regenerate us. From that time on, we have the indwelling of the Holy Spirit; this is the second step. Then, as He dwells within us, He is expecting to fill us. We are regenerated, and we have the indwelling of the Holy Spirit, but we need the infilling as something further. Regeneration, indwelling, and infilling are the inward aspects of the work of the Holy Spirit. We should discern the inner aspect of the work of the Holy Spirit from the outward aspect. We should never confuse them; to confuse them is terrible.

The Spirit in 1 Corinthians 12:13

The two aspects of the work of the Holy Spirit can be seen in 1 Corinthians 12:13, which says, "For also in one Spirit we were all baptized into one Body, whether Jews or Greeks, whether slaves or free, and were all given to drink one Spirit." To be baptized in one Spirit is one aspect, and to drink one Spirit is the other aspect. Both aspects are illustrated by water, but one aspect is to go into the water, while the other aspect is that the water comes into us. To be baptized in water is to get into the water, while to drink water is to take the water into us; these are two different actions.

We may have the inward aspect of the Spirit—regeneration, indwelling, and infilling—but we may not have the outward aspect of the Spirit. In the Old Testament, however, some people had the outward aspect without the inward aspect. We may have the drink within but not the clothing without, or we may have the clothing without but not the drink within. These are two different aspects, and neither can substitute for the other.

TWO KINDS OF FILLING WITH THE HOLY SPIRIT

There are two kinds of filling with the Holy Spirit, the inward filling and the outward filling, which are illustrated by water. To be filled with water as our drink is an inward filling. To be put into water to be baptized by immersion is an outward filling; to be buried, immersed, in water, is to be filled outwardly with the water.

In order to discern the two aspects of the work of the Spirit, we must point out a problem with translation. In the New Testament there are two different Greek words used for the filling of the Holy Spirit. In English, however, they are translated into the same word; this causes people to be unclear about this matter. In the New Testament there is always a distinction between these two fillings, and they are never confused.

Acts 2:2 says, "And suddenly there was a sound out of heaven, as of a rushing violent wind, and it filled the whole house where they were sitting." *Filled* here is the inward filling. This word in Greek is *pleroo,* meaning "to fill inwardly." In this verse, the wind filled the house inwardly. Verse 4 says, "And they were all filled with the Holy Spirit." The word *filled* here is another word in Greek, *pletho,* meaning "to fill outwardly." The wind filled the house inwardly, while the Holy Spirit filled the disciples outwardly. We may compare this to water in a baptistery. The baptistery is filled with water inwardly, but when someone is baptized in the baptistery, he is filled with the water not inwardly but outwardly.

Pleroo is used in Acts 13:52, which says, "And the disciples were filled with joy and with the Holy Spirit." It is also used in Ephesians 5:18, which says, "Be filled in spirit." This is the inward filling. The word *pletho* is used in Luke 1:15, 41, and 67, referring to John the Baptist, his mother, and his father, who were filled with the Spirit outwardly. This same word is used also in Acts 4:8 and 31, when the Spirit came upon Peter and the disciples. In 9:17 and 13:9 the Spirit also came upon Paul outwardly. *Pletho* in all these passages refers to the outpouring of the Spirit for the outward filling.

THE OUTWARD FILLING FOR MINISTRY

Luke 1:15 says, "For he will be great in the sight of the Lord, and he shall by no means drink wine and liquor. And he will be filled with the Holy Spirit, even from his mother's womb." This filling is the outward filling. For John the Baptist to be filled with the Holy Spirit outwardly means that the Holy Spirit would come down upon him to equip and empower him for his ministry. Verse 41 says, "And when Elizabeth heard Mary's greeting, the baby leaped in her womb, and Elizabeth was filled with the Holy Spirit." When Mary, the mother of the Lord, came to the mother of John the Baptist, the Holy Spirit came upon Elizabeth. She was filled outwardly with the Holy Spirit, so she prophesied. Verse 67 says, "And Zachariah his father was filled with the Holy Spirit and prophesied." The Holy Spirit came down also upon the father of John the Baptist, so he also prophesied. This was not the inward filling; it was the outward filling.

As we have seen, Acts 2:4 says that on the day of Pentecost, the disciples were in the house, which was filled with the Holy Spirit as the rushing wind, and they were all filled outwardly with the Holy Spirit. That is, they were baptized in the Holy Spirit on the day of Pentecost. To be baptized is to get into something, not to take something into us; this is the outward filling.

Acts 4:8 says, "Then Peter, filled with the Holy Spirit, said to them, Rulers of the people and elders." This filling was for power. At that time, Peter was empowered, equipped, with the Holy Spirit. He had received the outward filling on the day of Pentecost, but at this time the Holy Spirit came down upon him once more. In verse 31, Peter with the disciples was filled for a third time: "And when they had so besought, the place in which they were gathered was shaken, and they were all filled with the Holy Spirit and began to speak the word of God with boldness." They were filled outwardly with the Holy Spirit for power, not for life; this filling was something coming down upon them.

Acts 9:17 says, "And Ananias went away and entered into the house; and laying his hands on him, he said, Saul, brother, the Lord has sent me—Jesus, who appeared to you on the road on which you were coming—so that you may receive your sight and be filled with the Holy Spirit." A little disciple laid his hands on Saul, who later became the apostle Paul, that Saul might be filled with the Holy Spirit outwardly. Acts 13:9 says, "But Saul, who is also Paul, filled with the Holy Spirit, looked intently at him." On all the above occasions, this kind of filling was the outward filling for ministry.

TWO EXPERIENCES OF FILLING

By all these verses we can be clear about the two kinds of filling: the inward filling and the outward filling. The inward filling is for life, and the outward filling is for power in the ministry. The Lord Jesus was born of the Holy Spirit, so we must believe that He was filled inwardly with the Holy Spirit. However, at the age of thirty, before He came out to minister, He was baptized in the water, and the Holy Spirit came down upon Him as a dove. His inward filling and His outward filling were two different experiences. It was the same in principle with the apostles, such as Peter and John. On the day of resurrection, they received the Holy Spirit of life within them. It was many days later, however, on the day of Pentecost, that the Holy Spirit came down upon them, but before this day they had the Holy Spirit within them already.

When Saul, who later became the apostle Paul, was on the way to Damascus, he was met by the Lord. At that very moment he repented, he received the Lord Jesus as his Savior, and the Holy Spirit came into him. It is not logical to say that he received the Lord but did not receive the Holy Spirit within. Logically speaking, it must have been that when he was met by the Lord, he received the Lord, and at that very juncture the Holy Spirit came into him. Then after a certain period of time, the Lord sent a disciple named Ananias to lay hands on him so that he might be filled outwardly. This does not mean, however, that before that time Saul did not have the Holy Spirit within him. Paul's being filled with the Holy Spirit inwardly and outwardly were two different aspects.

THE CONDITION OF BEING FILLED INWARDLY

The adjective form of *pleroo* is *pleres,* referring to the condition after one has been filled with the Spirit inwardly. It is used in Luke 4:1, which says, "And Jesus, full of the Holy Spirit, returned from the Jordan and was led by the Spirit in the wilderness, while being tempted for forty days by the devil." The Lord Jesus was full of the Holy Spirit within. This is a matter of life. Similarly, Acts 6:3 says, "But brothers, look for seven well-attested men from among you, full of the Spirit and of wisdom, whom we will appoint over this need." Their being full was inward, not outward. Verse 5 continues, "And the word pleased all the multitude; and they chose Stephen, a man full of faith and of the Holy Spirit." *Full* here also refers to something within for life. Acts 7:55 also says that Stephen was full of the Holy Spirit within, and Acts 11:24 says of Barnabas, "For he was a good man and full of the Holy Spirit and of faith." This also is an inward filling for life. All these passages make it easy to realize that there are two aspects of the work of the Spirit: the inward filling and the outward filling.

FIVE CASES OF THE OUTWARD FILLING

In the book of Acts there are five particular cases of the outward filling. The first case was on the day of Pentecost. On that day, the Holy Spirit came down upon the disciples, and they were filled with the Spirit outwardly.

The second case was with the group of believers in Samaria, in Acts 8. Verse 15 says of Peter and John, "Who went down and prayed for them so that they might receive the Holy Spirit," and verse 17 says, "Then they laid their hands on them, and they received the Holy Spirit." These Samaritans were believers; they already had believed in the Lord Jesus. Therefore, it is impossible that they had not received the Holy Spirit within. For what then did the apostles Peter and John pray? It was for the outward work of the Holy Spirit. The Samaritans had received the Holy Spirit inwardly as life, but they had not received the Holy Spirit outwardly as power. Therefore, the apostles laid hands on them, the Holy Spirit came down upon them, and they received the Holy Spirit. If we read this passage carefully, we can see that it speaks of the Spirit upon them, not in them. As far as the Spirit being within them is concerned, this work was fully accomplished. They already had received the Spirit as life, but they had not received the Spirit coming down upon them as power.

The third case was the case of the apostle Paul, of which we have spoken already.

The fourth case was in the house of Cornelius in Acts 10:44-47. While Peter was speaking there, the Holy Spirit came upon the audience.

The fifth case is in Acts 19, with the believers in Ephesus. Verse 6 says, "And when Paul laid his hands on them, the Holy Spirit came upon them, and they spoke in tongues and prophesied." This does not mean that before this time these believers did not have the Holy Spirit within them. Before this time, at the time they received the Lord, they had received the Holy Spirit within them, but they had not yet received the Holy Spirit coming down upon them. In verse 2 Paul asked them, "Did you receive the Holy Spirit when you believed?" Paul did not mean that when these believers believed in the Lord, they did not receive the Holy Spirit within.

This was a word spoken to the disciples in Ephesus, and in Ephesians 1:13-14 Paul says clearly that at the time we believe in the Lord Jesus, we receive the Spirit within. If we compare Acts 19 with Ephesians 1, we can see that what the apostle asked about was not something inward but outward. The Ephesians had received the Holy Spirit within at the very time they believed in the Lord Jesus, but they had not received the Holy Spirit coming down upon them. By all these passages we can be very clear that the Holy Spirit within us for the inward filling is one matter, while the Holy Spirit upon us for the outward filling is another. These are two kinds of filling.

THE WAY TO BE FILLED INWARDLY

Now we must see the way to be filled. In order to fill a bottle or a cup with water, we must first empty it to make room for the water. We have the Holy Spirit dwelling within us; now it is a matter of whether or not we give Him the room within us. If we give Him the room, He will fill us. If we do not give Him the room, He will not fill us. The more we love the Lord and the more we give Him the room in us, the more the Holy Spirit will fill us.

Moreover, to be filled is not absolute; it is comparative. It is doubtful that we are absolutely filled within, but we may be filled to a comparative degree. Today we may feel that we are filled with the Holy Spirit within, but tomorrow we may realize that we are not yet filled; there is still some part not filled. Some part within us is occupied by something other than the Lord, something other than the Spirit.

The more room we give to the Lord, the more the Holy Spirit will fill us. We need to constantly be filled with the Holy Spirit. This means that we always need to give all the room within us to the Holy Spirit. We must have nothing other than the Lord occupying us, and we must not seek anything but the Lord Himself. Then we will be filled within. Why must we consecrate ourselves? It is simply to give all the room to the Lord. Why must we deal with so many sinful things? It is simply that we may give the room to the Lord so that He may fill us with the inward Spirit. Being filled depends on our giving room to the Holy Spirit.

THE WAY TO BE FILLED OUTWARDLY

By the Accomplished Baptism in the Holy Spirit

In two of the five cases in Acts—the first at Pentecost (2:4) and the fourth at the house of Cornelius (10:44-47)—there was no laying on of hands, but in three cases—the second, third, and fifth—there was the laying on of hands. The Spirit's speaking in Acts is that what happened on the day of Pentecost was the baptism of the Holy Spirit, and what happened in the house of Cornelius was also the baptism of the Holy Spirit (1:5; 11:15-17). Only these two cases are called the baptism in the Holy Spirit. The case on the day of Pentecost was the baptism of the Jewish believers, and the case in the house of Cornelius was the baptism of the Gentile believers. By these two cases the Lord as the Head of the Body baptized the entire Body into the Holy Spirit.

Therefore, the baptism in the Holy Spirit is absolutely an accomplished fact, just as the crucifixion of the Lord is an accomplished fact. After the Lord ascended to the heavens, He baptized the first part, the Jewish part, of His Body into the Holy Spirit on the day of Pentecost. Then in the house of Cornelius, He baptized the other part, the Gentile part, into the Spirit. By doing this, the Lord as the Head already has baptized His entire Body into the Holy Spirit. Thus, the baptism in the Holy Spirit is an accomplished fact.

When we preach the gospel, we must preach in this way. The Lord was incarnated as a man, bringing God into man. Then He was crucified on the cross to bear our sins so that we may be forgiven. Then He resurrected to impart His life to us so that we could have His life. After this, He ascended and poured down the Holy Spirit upon His Body so that we could have the baptism of the Holy Spirit. By His crucifixion and resurrection we have forgiveness of sins and eternal life, and by His ascension we have the Holy Spirit. The Lord has accomplished all these things, and this is the gospel.

By a Proper Standing with the Body

We must realize that the baptism in the Holy Spirit has been accomplished in the Body, the church. In order to share in this baptism as a member of the Body, we must be right with the Body. This is the principle of the laying on of hands. The Body has been baptized into the Holy Spirit, the Holy Spirit is now upon the Body, and now we have become members of the Body. Therefore, we need a representative member of the Body to contact us so that the Holy Spirit on the Body can come upon us through that contact. This is why we need another member of the Body to lay hands on us. When a member representing the Body contacts us, the oil upon the Body flows onto us.

The principle here is that we must be right with the Body. If we simply get right with the Body, it is easy to experience the baptism of the Holy Spirit. Whenever we need it, we can simply claim it and take it. The baptism in the Spirit already has been accomplished on the Body, the Spirit is upon the Body, and we are members of the Body. If we are right with the Body, we can claim this baptism by faith.

Do not ask me what the evidences or manifestations of this fact will be. I do not want to tell you, because I do not know what they will be for you. However, I am sure that you will have certain manifestations. If we have a right relationship with the Body and if we stand in the right position, claiming it and receiving it by faith, we will experience the baptism in the Holy Spirit. This is the right way.

Sometimes we experience the baptism in the Holy Spirit with certain kinds of feelings. However, it is still a matter of faith. We may be about to minister, to preach. At that time we realize that the baptism of the Holy Spirit has been accomplished on the Body already. The Holy Spirit has poured Himself upon the Body, and we are members of the Body, so we make our relationship with the Body right, and we stand in this right position, claiming this baptism and taking it by faith. If we do this, then when we preach, we will preach in power. It does not matter whether or not we feel it; we will still preach powerfully. Sometimes the Lord does give us a feeling, and we can sense the baptism, but whether or not we sense it, we have the liberty and the release. When we are in the Holy Spirit and under the power of the Spirit, we have liberty, boldness, and release.

The laying on of hands is not a form. It is a principle. The principle is to get right with the Body. If we are not right with the Body, then even if someone comes and lays hands upon us, this will not work. In this case, it is only a form. The principle is to realize that the Holy Spirit has been poured down upon the Body, and today the Holy Spirit from the Lord as the Head is upon the Body already. Now we have become members of the Body, we are right with the Body, and we take this standing and claim it by faith. Then we will have the baptism. This is a matter of faith based upon what the Lord has accomplished.

In my many years of ministry, I can testify that at least once, while I was ministering on the platform in 1935, I did sense the outpouring of the Holy Spirit. It was like a cloud coming down upon me. While I was ministering, I was in a room, but I was also in the cloud. Many times I have sensed something in a different way. However, there is no need to pay attention to this sense. We should simply get right with the Body and take the standing that we are members of the Body. We should claim this fact with the saints.

We have the outpouring. Do you believe this? Do not listen to the other voices, which say that we must tarry, fast, cry, or even roll, jump, or exercise our mouth to speak in tongues in order to receive the outpouring. Some say you must jump up and down before you are filled with the Holy Spirit. Others say you must roll, laugh, or twist your tongue to make strange utterances. I cannot find such things in the Scriptures. I know about these practices, and I have seen them. I am not against anything genuine or real, but I must tell you the truth. The right way to receive the outpouring is to have a proper standing with the Body and to claim it by faith.

All these things have been accomplished by the Lord. He died, resurrected, and ascended. By His death He dealt with our sins; by His resurrection He imparted Himself as life to us; and in His ascension He has poured down His Spirit upon His Body. This is the gospel. Now we must simply receive it by faith. If we say, "Lord, I thank You that You died for me on the cross," all our sins are forgiven. If we say, "Lord, You have been resurrected, so I take You as my life," we have eternal life. In the same way, we must take the fact, saying, "Lord, You have ascended to the heavens and have poured down Your Spirit upon the Body. Lord, I am a member of that Body, and I have the standing, the liberty, and the right to claim what You have poured down." This is the gospel, and we should happily receive it by faith.

We must realize that all these things have been accomplished by the Lord. Everything is ours. There is no need to tarry, cry, shout, laugh, roll, jump, or dance. We simply take them by faith. However, in order to exercise faith, we must have the right position and stand upon it.

CHAPTER THREE

THE MANIFESTATION OF THE HOLY SPIRIT

Scripture Reading: 1 Cor. 12:7-11

We have seen clearly from the teachings of the Scriptures that the work of the Holy Spirit is of two different aspects. One aspect is that the Holy Spirit comes into us and dwells within us. The other aspect is that the Holy Spirit comes down upon us. The Holy Spirit within us as life is the inward aspect, and the Holy Spirit upon us as power is the outward aspect. In order to be clear about the work of the Holy Spirit, we must differentiate these two aspects. Moreover, we must know that the Holy Spirit as life dwells within us to be the Spirit of life, the Spirit of reality, the seal which seals us as the inheritance of God, and the pledge to guarantee that all that God is and God has is our portion. In addition, this Spirit dwells within us to be the very Paraclete, the Comforter, the One who takes care of us in our daily life. These are the different items of the work of the Holy Spirit as life within us.

THE NEED FOR THE HOLY SPIRIT
AS POWER AND RELEASE

The Spirit also comes upon us as power. We may have the Spirit within us as life, yet it is very possible that we have not experienced the Holy Spirit as power upon us. In order to have a proper life and walk as a Christian, we need the Holy Spirit within us as life day by day, even moment by moment. By the Holy Spirit within us as life, we may have a very nice, spiritual Christian walk and daily life. However, we may still be very weak in the service. We may have a very spiritual daily walk, yet when we go to preach the gospel to people, we find that we are weak. Our preaching of the gospel is often weak. We feel that we are bound by something; we are not released, and we do not have the boldness, the encouragement, to speak something for the Lord. We are nice and spiritual in our daily Christian walk, but we are weak in the service, in the preaching of the gospel, and in the ministry. This proves that although we have the Holy Spirit within us as life, we do not have the Holy Spirit upon us as power.

This is not merely a theory. This can be proved by many cases. Throughout my life I have met many nice Christians who are spiritual in their life and walk. However, I realize, and even they themselves realize, that they are very weak in the Lord's service, in gospel preaching, in winning souls, and in the ministry of the word. They are weak because they lack the Holy Spirit upon them as power. They have the first aspect of the work of the Holy Spirit, but they do not have the second aspect.

Consider the Lord Jesus. When He came out to preach the gospel for God at the age of thirty, He needed to be baptized. Then the Holy Spirit came down upon Him as the dove so that He might be empowered to preach the gospel. He needed to be anointed outwardly by the Holy Spirit to have the power for preaching.

The principle is the same with the disciples on the day of Pentecost. Before that day, the disciples already had the Holy Spirit within them as life, but they did not have the Holy Spirit upon them as power. Therefore, after they had received the Spirit of life within, the Lord told them to tarry, to wait, in Jerusalem until the day the Spirit would be poured out upon them as power. After that time, on the day of Pentecost, Peter and the other apostles did not manifest how much life they had or how spiritual they were. Rather, they manifested how powerful they were.

To be spiritual is one thing, but to be powerful is another. We can be very spiritual in life. We can know how to discern the soul from the spirit, and we may know how to walk and do things in the spirit and not the soul. However, we may be weak in preaching, ministry, and service. Therefore, we need power. We need the outpouring, not only the infilling, of the Holy Spirit. The infilling of the Spirit is for our spiritual life, while the outpouring of the Spirit upon us is for spiritual service. On the day of Pentecost, Peter and the other disciples were powerful because on that day they received the Spirit coming down upon them as power.

The Holy Spirit upon us is not only for power but for release. We cannot find the word *release* used in this way in the New Testament, but we can demonstrate it by the experience of many saints. When we have the Holy Spirit coming down upon us, we are released from all bondage, care, and fear. If we have the Holy Spirit upon us, we have the boldness to utter and release whatever we feel in our spirit. But if we do not have the Holy Spirit upon us, even if we have something spiritual, heavenly, and divine in our spirit, we do not have the liberty, the release, and the boldness to release it.

A brother may love the Lord very much and walk in the spirit. He may be a truly spiritual person, but he may not have the Spirit upon him. Therefore, when he has the opportunity to speak for the Lord to others, he is very reluctant and afraid to speak. He does not have the boldness, and he is limited. He has much within, but very little without to utter or express. It seems that he is fearful of something. This is due to the lack of the power and the release of the Holy Spirit. If we have the Holy Spirit upon us, we have release and boldness.

Everyone who has the Holy Spirit upon him does not care about his face. He has the boldness and the release to speak everything that he feels within. This is why when we go to preach the gospel, we need the Holy Spirit not only as power but as release. I was saved when I was less than twenty years old through the preaching of a young sister who was less than twenty-five years old. In all the campaigns she had, there were always more than one thousand people. She was a young Chinese girl who did not even finish high school, but whenever she stood to speak she did not regard any man, no matter how old or big he was. She came as a judge with boldness for utterance. Her speaking was even terrifying because she had the Holy Spirit upon her not only as power but also as her release. If you would go to her after her preaching, you could see that she was simply a small, quiet young woman, but when she went to the platform, her whole person and everything within her was released. She had the full release and liberty.

POWER, RELEASE, AND GIFTS
AS THE MANIFESTATION OF THE SPIRIT

When the Holy Spirit comes upon us, there is a manifestation. Each of the nine gifts in 1 Corinthians 12:7-10 is a different manifestation of the Holy Spirit upon us. However, we must be careful. This does not mean that if we do not have one of these nine gifts, we do not have the Holy Spirit upon us. We may have the Holy Spirit coming down upon us as power, yet we may not have any of these nine gifts.

More than one person has told me that they can speak in tongues by themselves without the Holy Spirit coming upon them. One Caucasian brother demonstrated to me and a second brother, who also spoke Chinese, how he could speak in a Chinese dialect in this way. After speaking, he asked us if we could understand it, and we replied that we could not. Then he began to speak in another tone of voice. He spoke in four or five ways, but we could not understand him. We could understand all the leading dialects of Chinese, but we could not understand what this brother said. His speaking in tongues was absolutely false. If someone can exercise to speak in tongues by himself without having the Spirit, it is not genuine. Speaking in tongues is a manifestation of the Holy Spirit coming upon us. Without the Holy Spirit coming upon us, how can we speak in another tongue? If speaking in many tongues is a matter of merely changing our tone of voice, that is ridiculous.

Speaking in tongues must be by a miraculous power from the Holy Spirit. If one can speak in tongues at any time by himself, it is human-manufactured. It is not by the outpouring of the power of the Holy Spirit. The genuine speaking in tongues must be something in the power of the Holy Spirit. If the Spirit comes down upon us like burning electricity, our speaking in tongues is miraculous and truly genuine. We cannot exercise to speak in tongues in a genuine way at any time without having the Holy Spirit coming upon us.

To be sure, when the Holy Spirit comes upon us, we will have power. If we have something other than power, we should not believe it, because the main purpose for the Holy Spirit coming upon us is for power. Regrettably, I have seen many persons who spoke in tongues but did not have power. Therefore, I am dubious that this kind of speaking was genuine. The genuine speaking in tongues must be in power.

We may have the power of the Holy Spirit, yet we may not have one of the nine gifts in 1 Corinthians 12. Verses 7-11 say, "But to each one is given the manifestation of the Spirit for what is profitable. For to one through the Spirit a word of wisdom is given, and to another a word of knowledge, according to the same Spirit; to a different one faith in the same Spirit, and to another gifts of healing in the one Spirit, and to another operations of works of power, and to another prophecy, and to another discerning of spirits; to a different one various kinds of tongues, and to another interpretation of tongues. But the one and the same Spirit operates all these things, distributing to each one respectively even as He purposes." Here there is no hint that these nine gifts are the only manifestation of the Spirit. In the same chapter, verse 28 says, "And God has placed some in the church: first apostles." This verse speaks of apostles, but verses 7-11 mention nothing about apostles. Therefore, we should not think that the nine gifts in these verses are all the manifestations or the only manifestations. Besides these nine gifts there are other aspects of the manifestation of the Spirit.

The preaching of the gospel, for example, is not included in these nine gifts. I saw a number of brothers in China that were very powerful and prevailing in the preaching of the gospel, yet they never spoke in tongues or prophesied miraculously. One of them was Dr. John Sun. Thousands of people were brought to the Lord through him. Not only did certain powerful brothers not speak in tongues, but they were opposed to it. I do not agree with their opposition; they opposed too much. Nevertheless, although they did not agree with speaking in tongues, they were very powerful in the preaching of the gospel. I went to their meetings several times when I was young. Their speaking about the Lord was powerful. There is no doubt that the Holy Spirit was there. Is this not a manifestation of the Holy Spirit? To be sure, it is.

When the Spirit comes upon us, we first have power. Second we have release, and third we have a gift as a manifestation, such as one of the nine gifts in 1 Corinthians 12. However, these nine gifts are not the only gifts, the only manifestation, of the Spirit. We can prove this by the experiences of the saints. We may have one of these nine gifts, or we may have some other manifestation. How can we know that we have the Holy Spirit upon us? It is by the power, release, and some sort of gift.

We must be very clear that the Holy Spirit upon us is for power. When we have the Holy Spirit upon us, we are empowered and released. The purpose of the Holy Spirit coming down upon us outwardly is for power and gifts. We may compare power to gasoline in a car. If we do not have gasoline, we do not have power for our car. Gifts, on the other hand, are a technical ability. We may have a car with power, but we may not have the ability to drive. The ability to drive is a gift.

I have seen many brothers who had both the power and the gift to preach the gospel. When I first met Brother Watchman Nee, I realized that he had the gift of teaching. Later I realized that he also had the gift of preaching. His preaching was more a matter of gift than power. Once, a number of brothers were dealing with an unbelieving schoolmate, doing their best to convince him and win his soul. They could not do it, so they came to Brother Nee. He told them to bring the classmate to him. They were happy to do so, and they all came to see what would happen. After only a few minutes, that man was saved. To be sure, Brother Nee had a gift.

Sometimes when the Spirit comes upon someone, He endues him with a certain gift, a spiritual "technical" ability, to do a work in the spiritual realm. When Brother Watchman Nee was young, he preached in Nanking to some university students. After his preaching, a thoughtful young man came to him and said, "I am very influenced by your preaching. I have the desire to believe in the very Jesus Christ whom you preach. However, I have a problem I wish for you to solve. My parents are old and are strong in Buddhism. To be sure, they will oppose my becoming a Christian. Therefore, I must wait until they die. Then I will become a Christian. Mr. Nee, do you agree with me about this?" Brother Nee was very skillful. He spoke a simple, brief word in a very solemn attitude, saying, "Do you honor your parents so much that you wish to send them to hell first, and then you will go to heaven?" In tears the young man said, "Mr. Nee, I must believe in the Lord Jesus and open the way to bring my parents to heaven." This simple word took only one minute. Brother Nee had a gift; he knew how to handle such a person. Others do not have such a gift. They are like someone who ruins an appliance by handling it the wrong way.

When the Holy Spirit comes upon us, we may not have a special manifestation, but we will have a gift, especially for gospel preaching. That also is a kind of manifestation. The Holy Spirit within us is for life and as life, and the Holy Spirit upon us is for power and gift. If we do not have power and gift, but rather do many foolish things, we do not have the Holy Spirit upon us. If we have the Holy Spirit upon us, we will have power and an effective gift.

THE MANIFESTATION OF THE SPIRIT IN THE FIVE CASES IN ACTS

We may now come back to the five cases of receiving the Spirit outwardly in the book of Acts. In the first case, all the disciples were powerful on the day of Pentecost, and they had the release, boldness, and encouragement. They dared to speak as the Lord led. They also had the gifts; they spoke in tongues, in different human languages. Peter and the others also had the gift of preaching. Before the day of Pentecost, Peter spoke foolishly many times. Only once, in Matthew 16:16, did Peter speak clearly according to the heavenly vision. He recognized the Lord as the Christ, the Son of the living God. This was the clearest and most accurate word he spoke. Besides this, whatever he spoke was often foolish. However, his message on the day of Pentecost was wonderful. It was clear, powerful, and given in a good way. At that time he received the gift of preaching. He had not only the power to preach but also the gift to present the gospel in a good, effective, prevailing, and brief way in a good order. This was the sermon, the message, given by Peter, an unlearned fisherman, who received a gift.

In the second case, the case of the Samaritan believers in Acts 8, there is nothing concerning speaking in tongues. However, people could see that the believers had the Holy Spirit upon them. There must have been certain signs which people saw that indicated that the Spirit was upon them. Some today may insist that what they saw was speaking in tongues. However, the Holy Spirit in composing Acts 8 does not mention speaking in tongues, and what the Scriptures do not say may be more meaningful than what they do say. There is nothing mentioned by the Spirit about speaking in tongues, yet people saw that the Holy Spirit came down upon the saints. Many times I have seen people receive the Holy Spirit upon them without speaking in tongues. There is some kind of sign by which we know the Holy Spirit is upon a person.

The third case is concerning Saul, who later became the apostle Paul. Shortly after he was saved, a disciple, a believer by the name of Ananias, came to him and laid hands on him, and Saul received the Holy Spirit. In this case, nothing more is mentioned. The Scriptures in Acts 9 only tell us that the Holy Spirit came upon Saul. Later, the apostle Paul said that he spoke in tongues more than others (1 Cor. 14:18), but when he received the Holy Spirit upon him, the record of the Scriptures says nothing about speaking in tongues. Therefore, we should not insist that speaking in tongues is the initial evidence of the Holy Spirit. We have at least the two cases of the Samaritan believers and of Saul, in which the Scriptures do not mention speaking in tongues.

The fourth case is concerning the house of Cornelius. This case is very wonderful. At the time the people in that house were regenerated, they all received the Holy Spirit upon them, and they spoke in tongues (Acts 10:44-46). The people there received almost everything. They received the Holy Spirit within as life, and at the same time they received the Holy Spirit without as power. They received life, they received power, and they received a gift. This is the normal case. In the normal condition, a person is saved in the way of the house of

Cornelius. At the same time the Holy Spirit comes into him as life to regenerate him, He comes upon him as power. Then this person has life within and power and gift without. However, the experience of many believers is not normal.

The fifth case is concerning a small group of believers in Ephesus. When the apostle Paul came to them, he laid his hands on them, the Holy Spirit came upon them, and they spoke in tongues (19:6). They had speaking in tongues as the manifestation of the Spirit.

We have the Holy Spirit within as life and without as power and gift. If we are truly filled with the Holy Spirit within, we have the riches of the life of the Lord. If we do not have the riches of the spiritual life, this proves that although we have the Holy Spirit dwelling within us, we are not filled with Him. In the same way, if we have the Holy Spirit upon us, we have power and a certain kind of gift. We cannot say that we have the Holy Spirit upon us if we are not powerful and are unable to do anything. We must have power and gift.

All of the above show us the two aspects of the work of the Holy Spirit. However, we must realize that these are not aspects of the work of two Spirits. They are different aspects of the work of the one Holy Spirit.

THE NEED FOR A COMPLETE EXPERIENCE
OF THE SPIRIT

As Christians we must experience the Holy Spirit in regeneration, infilling, power, and gifts. If we have only regeneration, we are merely at the beginning of being a Christian. Inwardly we need to be filled with the Holy Spirit, and outwardly we need power and gift. If we do not have power and gift, we are not complete in the experience of the Holy Spirit.

The experience of the baptism of the Holy Spirit is the last item of the experience of the Spirit. The Lord gives us the Holy Spirit first for regeneration, then for infilling, and then for power and gift, or simply stated, for baptism. On the one hand, we must be regenerated with the Spirit and filled with the Spirit, and on the other hand, we must be baptized in the Spirit. To be baptized in the Spirit means that we are not only filled with the Spirit, but we are absolutely in the Spirit. Inwardly we are filled with the Spirit, and outwardly we are in the Spirit. In this way we have life, and we have power and gift. Then we are normal Christians.

We should not merely say, "Praise the Lord, I have been regenerated and filled to some degree by the Holy Spirit. Now I love the Lord, I walk in the Spirit, and I am more or less spiritual. I am satisfied as a good Christian." We may be a very good brother or sister, but do we have power, release, and a certain kind of gift? The only way to experience the baptism of the Holy Spirit is to stand in the position of being a member of the Body to claim the Spirit, who has been poured upon the Body. In this way we will experience the baptism of the Holy Spirit; we will be empowered, and we will be gifted.

What we are saying here is very general and according to the holy Scriptures. I do not say that you must speak in tongues. Perhaps the Lord will give you this gift, but I do not say that this must be the initial evidence of the Spirit. Rather, speaking in tongues is only one of many aspects of the manifestation of the Spirit. The Spirit upon us is for power and gifts, not for anything peculiar. Do not look for something peculiar; rather, seek the experience of power and gifts.

Many of us read the Scriptures, but if we receive the outpouring of the Holy Spirit upon us as power and the means for gift, we will have a new way to understand the Scriptures. We will understand the old book in a new way; that is, we will have the gift to understand the Scriptures. On the one hand, we do not have the scriptural ground to speak of "the gift of reading," but on the other hand, we should not be too technical and legal about words.

Similarly, as brothers and sisters we love the Lord, and we are concerned about the church, the saints, and the souls of others. However, some say, "I am too weak, and I can do nothing. I am concerned about the saints, but when I go to them, I do not know what to say or what to do." I fully sympathize with you, but I wish to tell you that if you experience the baptism of the Holy Spirit, you will immediately know how to contact people. You will have the power, the boldness, and the gift to contact them. I cannot show you where the Scriptures speak of "the gift of visitation," but I can tell you that if you have the experience of the baptism of the Holy Spirit, you will be able to contact persons. You will have not only the power but also the way, the gift, and the technical ability to contact them.

Many times when we come to the meetings, we have a heart to express something in prayer, but when the time comes to pray, we are weak and we simply do not have the way to pray. Instead, we have many excuses not to pray. However, if we would experience the baptism of the Holy Spirit, when we come to the meeting, we will have the power and the gift to pray. Again, I cannot find the ground in the Scriptures that there is "the gift of prayer." On the one hand, prayer is not a gift, but on the other hand, in order to have the way to pray and to pray in the right way, we should experience the baptism of the Holy Spirit. After the experience of the baptism of the Holy Spirit, we will have a prevailing way to pray.

With all spiritual things—service, preaching, reading, and prayer—there is the need of the outpouring of the Holy Spirit upon us. It is not sufficient only to have the Holy Spirit within us; we need the Holy Spirit upon us. Do not say, "As long as I have the Holy Spirit within me, that is good enough. I simply do not care for the so-called Pentecostal activities." We can forget about the so-called Pentecostal activities, but we must realize that the Holy Spirit is not only for us inwardly as life but also outwardly as power and gift.

SEEKING TO MAKE UP OUR SHORTNESS

Do we have these two aspects? We need the outward experience of the Holy Spirit, to experience the Holy Spirit as power and as the Giver. If we only have the Holy Spirit within and we never experience the Holy Spirit without, we are short. We are not complete in the experience of the Holy Spirit. The last step of the work of the Holy Spirit is the baptism, the outpouring, the outward aspect. We must experience the Holy Spirit as power with gift to us. On the one hand, we must seek to be filled with the Spirit within, and on the other hand, we must seek to be filled by the Holy Spirit as power with different kinds of gifts without.

I present this to you as a clear picture of our situation so that we may know where we are and what we are short of. May the Lord enable us to seek, to make up, what we are short of. We should forget about the different situations, different speakings, and different teachings in today's Christianity concerning this matter. Let us come back to the Scriptures in a simple and clear way to see that the Holy Spirit is within us for life and upon us for power with gift.

We must know what we have experienced and what we have not experienced, what we have and what we are short of. May the Lord be merciful to us that we may seek what we are short of and make it up. We need the inward filling of the Spirit and also the outward filling, that is, the Holy Spirit as power with different kinds of gifts to us.

We need some time to be with the Lord to deal with this matter. We should also come together and pray about how to take the position and claim what the Body has received already, and how to experience the outpouring, the accomplished baptism, of the Holy Spirit on the Body, so that we may have the real experience of the Holy Spirit upon us as power with gift. Then we will be empowered, and we will be gifted. We will have not only life within but also power and gift without. In this way we will be normal Christians. On the one hand, we will be normal in life, and on the other hand, we will be normal in service. We must seek this, and we should not be satisfied with the present situation.

CHAPTER FOUR

MANY ASPECTS OF THE MANIFESTATION OF THE HOLY SPIRIT

Scripture Reading: Gal. 5:22-25; Eph. 4:2; Col. 3:12; 2 Pet 1:5-6; Rom. 14:17; Eph. 5:9; 4:24; Matt. 5:5-6, 8-9; 1 Cor. 12:4-10, 28; Mark 16:17-18; Heb. 2:4; Acts 2:16-18, 4-11; 10:44-46; 19:6

It is easy to realize how the Holy Spirit is life to us in our spirit, but it is more complicated to realize how the Spirit is upon us as power. Therefore, we must speak in more detail concerning this matter.

THE NEED FOR CAREFUL STUDY
CONCERNING SPEAKING IN TONGUES

One reason we must spend so much time to deal with this matter is that we need to see where speaking in tongues stands. Many people are careless in studying and understanding the Word simply because they are careless in their character. They are careless in all things, and when they come to the Word to study and understand it, they are still careless, even to the utmost degree. We must learn the lesson not to be careless. In order to be careful, we must build up our character. Then when we come to study the Word, we will understand it carefully.

The tongues movement began in the previous century in England, and it came to Los Angeles in 1906, two years after the Welsh revival, which was under the leadership of Evan Roberts. This revival influenced some people on the West Coast of the United States. At the start of this movement on the West Coast, they did not have speaking in tongues, but later tongues were brought in. There was also a movement with speaking in tongues on the East Coast. From that time on, speaking in tongues has been a big problem among the Lord's children in this country, which has not yet been settled. This matter disturbs the Lord's children very much, and to some extent, it frightens them away from seeking the real experience of the baptism of the Holy Spirit.

At first I had no thought to deal with this matter, but after I stayed in this country for a period of time, I found out that it is a real problem. Today many people pay much attention to speaking in tongues. Many insist on saying that speaking in tongues is the initial and necessary evidence of the baptism of the Holy Spirit. Since I came to this country, I have traveled much, and wherever I go people often ask me, "What about speaking in tongues? Do you speak in tongues?" I have been very surprised to hear this so much.

THE FRUIT OF THE SPIRIT

Now we must study the Word in a very careful way. Two particular chapters in the Scriptures speak of the Spirit. Galatians 5 deals with the Spirit as life within us, while 1 Corinthians 12 deals with the Spirit as power upon us.

Nine Items in Galatians 5:22-25

Galatians 5:22-25 says, "But the fruit of the Spirit is love, joy, peace, long-suffering, kindness, goodness, faithfulness, meekness, self-control; against such things there is no law. But they who are of Christ Jesus have crucified the flesh with its passions and its lusts. If we live by the Spirit, let us also walk by the Spirit." Verse 22 speaks not of the fruits of the Spirit but of the fruit, singular in number and with the singular verb *is*. The nine items mentioned in verses 22-23 are not nine fruits but nine aspects of the one fruit of the Spirit. These nine aspects start with love, end with self-control, and have joy, peace, long-suffering, kindness, goodness, faithfulness, and meekness in between.

These nine aspects are the fruit of the Spirit as life within us; they are not aspects of the Spirit as power upon us. We must note, however, that these nine aspects are not all the aspects of the fruit of the Spirit as some teach today in

Christianity. We can prove that there are other aspects not mentioned here.

More Items in the Gospels and the Epistles

The eighth item in Galatians 5, for example, is meekness, which in the Greek text is *prautes.* Ephesians 4:2 speaks of "all lowliness and meekness." Here *meekness* is the same Greek word as in Galatians 5:23. In addition to meekness, however, there is *lowliness,* which in Greek means "humility of mind." This is the same Greek word used in Philippians 2:3 and Colossians 3:12, which also mentions meekness. According to the text of these verses, lowliness and meekness are two different items. Galatians 5 speaks of meekness, but it does not mention lowliness or humility. Since lowliness is omitted from Galatians 5, the nine items mentioned there are not all the items of the fruit of the Spirit.

Second Peter 1:5-6 says, "And for this very reason also, adding all diligence, supply bountifully in your faith virtue; and in virtue, knowledge; and in knowledge, self-control; and in self-control, endurance; and in endurance, godliness." Galatians 5 speaks of self-control, but it does not speak of godliness. Godliness is in addition to the nine items there.

Romans 14:17 says, "For the kingdom of God is not eating and drinking, but righteousness and peace and joy in the Holy Spirit." Ephesians 5:9 also mentions righteousness and truth. Galatians 5, however, speaks of joy and peace but not of righteousness and truth. Moreover, in Ephesians 4:24 there is righteousness and holiness, but Galatians 5 does not mention holiness. In addition, Matthew 5:5 and 9 speak of meekness and peace, while verse 6 speaks of righteousness, and verse 8 speaks of purity. Galatians 5, however, mentions peace and meekness but not righteousness and purity.

According to the above verses, at least lowliness, godliness, righteousness, truth, holiness, and purity are not mentioned in Galatians 5. There is no reason to doubt that these also are items of the fruit of the Spirit. This proves that the nine items mentioned in this chapter are not all the aspects of the fruit of the Spirit. We should not believe that there are only nine aspects of the fruit of the Spirit as life within us. There are many more than nine. To think that there are only nine is to be careless. We must be careful in studying and understanding the Word. If we understand it carelessly, we will hinder ourselves and damage others.

Galatians 5 tells us that the Holy Spirit within us is the Spirit of life who brings forth spiritual fruit with many aspects, including the nine aspects mentioned here and others. The apostle's intention is not to tell us how many aspects of the fruit of the Spirit there are. There is no need to do this. His intention is to tell us the difference between the works of the flesh and the fruit of the Spirit as life within us. In order to do this, he illustrates by listing a certain number of the aspects of the fruit of the Spirit. Therefore, we should not say that the items of the fruit of the Spirit are only nine. Rather, we can clearly prove that there are more than nine.

All the foregoing prove how careless some people are in understanding the Scriptures. In some places, people list the nine items in Galatians 5 on a chart and call them the nine fruits. They say that all the fruits are nine in number; love is one fruit, joy is another fruit, peace is another fruit, long-suffering is another fruit, and so on. If we read carefully, however, we can see that these are not nine fruits but nine of the aspects of the one fruit. Moreover, there are other aspects not included here.

THE MANIFESTATION OF THE SPIRIT

Nine Items in 1 Corinthians 12

First Corinthians 12:4-6 says, "But there are distinctions of gifts, but the same Spirit; and there are distinctions of ministries, yet the same Lord; and there are distinctions of operations, but the same God, who operates all things in all." Gifts are of the Spirit, ministries are of the Lord, and operations are of God. This refers to the Triune God.

Verse 7 says, "But to each one is given the manifestation of the Spirit for what is profitable." *Gifts* in verse 4 is plural, while *manifestation* in verse 7 is singular. The gifts are many, but the manifestation is one. Just as the fruit of the Holy Spirit as life within us is one fruit with many aspects, in the same principle the manifestation of the Holy Spirit as power upon us is one manifestation with many aspects, which are the gifts mentioned in verses 8-10. These verses say, "For to one through the Spirit a word of wisdom is given, and to another a word of knowledge, according to the same Spirit; to a different one faith in the same Spirit, and to another gifts of healing in the one Spirit, and to another operations of works of power, and to another prophecy, and to another discerning of spirits; to a different one various kinds of tongues, and to another interpretation of tongues." The word of wisdom, for example, is not the manifestation of the Spirit but only one item of the manifestation.

It is remarkable that here again there are nine aspects. Galatians 5 mentions nine aspects of the fruit of the Holy Spirit as life within us, while this chapter speaks of nine aspects of the manifestation of the Holy Spirit as power upon us. The Spirit as life brings forth fruit, while the Holy Spirit as power has a manifestation. The fruit of life has many aspects, and the manifestation of power also has many aspects.

More Items in 1 Corinthians 12

However, are there only nine aspects of the manifestation of the Holy Spirit as power? Verse 28 says, "And God has placed some in the church: first apostles, second prophets, third teachers; then works of power, then gifts of healing, helps, administrations, various kinds of tongues." The nine aspects in verses 8-10 do not include helps and administrations, for example. Verse 28 also speaks of apostles and teachers, which we cannot find in verses 8-10. Verse 8 mentions the word of wisdom and the word of knowledge, but these may not include teaching. Of the items in verse 28, some are mentioned among the nine items, and some are not. It is clear that at least apostles, helps, and administrations are not included among the nine. Therefore, we cannot say that those nine items are all the items of the manifestation of the Holy Spirit.

More Items in Mark 16:17-18

Mark 16:17-18 says, "And these signs will accompany

those who believe: in My name they will cast out demons; they will speak with new tongues; they will pick up serpents; and if they drink anything deadly, it shall by no means harm them; they will lay hands on the sick, and they will be well." The first sign mentioned here is casting out demons. To be sure, this is an aspect of the manifestation of the Holy Spirit upon us as power; if someone casts out demons, he must be in the power of the Holy Spirit. However, this is not one of the nine items in 1 Corinthians 12. Of the five items mentioned in Mark 16, only two—speaking with new tongues and healing the sick—are included among the nine. The other three— casting out demons, picking up serpents, and drinking something deadly but not being harmed—are not included.

More Items in Hebrews 2:4

Hebrews 2:4 says, "God bearing witness with them both by signs and wonders and by various works of power and by distributions of the Holy Spirit according to His will." Only works of power and distributions of the Holy Spirit are included in 1 Corinthians 12. Signs and wonders are not included there. This is a strong proof that those nine items are not all the aspects of the manifestation of the Spirit. To be sure, casting out demons cannot be confused with any of the nine items; it is a separate item. Therefore, we should not believe that those nine are all the aspects. Besides those nine, there are others.

It is needless to say that if we do not have speaking in tongues, we can still have the manifestation of the Holy Spirit; even if we have none of those nine items, we still can have the manifestation of the Holy Spirit. Those today who insist that we must speak in tongues to prove we have the manifestation of the Holy Spirit are carelessly wrong, so wrong that they damage the Lord's people in this matter.

SPEAKING IN TONGUES
NOT BEING A NECESSARY MANIFESTATION

I have spent much time to study the Word and the present situation with respect to the so-called Pentecostal movement and speaking in tongues. I began to study in this way in July of 1932. At that time I visited one of the most prevailing Pentecostal movements in China. I stayed with those people, and I attended their meetings. By 1935 I myself had been helped in this matter, and I had the experience of speaking in tongues. In the following year, I helped many people also to speak in tongues. The first article I wrote on this subject was published in Chinese in 1936. It dealt with the two aspects of the work of the Holy Spirit and included something about speaking in tongues. By this you can see how long I have studied this matter. Through all this study I have become clear.

In the past more than twenty years, the churches in the Far East have practiced the way of the outward gifts several times, and we learned something from this experience. After much study I have learned that the entire Scriptures make it clear that speaking in tongues is not the initial evidence of the baptism of the Holy Spirit, and it is not a necessity. Speaking in tongues is only one of many aspects of the manifestation of the Holy Spirit as power upon us.

People such as the Brethren and other fundamental Christians say that speaking in tongues is something devilish. They insist that this kind of miraculous gift ended with the apostolic times, so that today there is no more speaking in tongues. I do not agree with this; they are too extreme. Up to today there is the real, genuine speaking in tongues. Yet I do not agree that speaking in tongues is the necessary and initial evidence of the baptism of the Holy Spirit. Speaking in tongues is only one of many aspects of the manifestation of the Holy Spirit. First Corinthians 12 clearly says that it is one of nine aspects, and as we have seen, these nine are not all the aspects. Besides these, there are other aspects, such as casting out demons.

Acts 2:16-18 says, "But this is what is spoken through the prophet Joel: 'And it shall be in the last days, says God, that I will pour out of My Spirit upon all flesh, and your sons and your daughters shall prophesy, and your young men shall see visions, and your old men shall dream things in dreams; and indeed upon My slaves, both men and women, I will pour out of My Spirit in those days, and they shall prophesy.'" Here are two additional items—visions and dreams—that are not listed among the nine in 1 Corinthians 12. On the day of Pentecost, Peter clearly said that in the last days the Lord would pour out His Spirit upon His people, and that some of them would prophesy, some would have visions, and some would dream things in dreams. Although the disciples on the day of Pentecost spoke in tongues, the prophecy of Joel mentions nothing about tongues. Nevertheless, Peter said concerning the day of Pentecost, "This is what is spoken through the prophet Joel."

Many people insist on speaking in tongues, but the prophet Joel did not insist on it. Rather, he said that some would prophesy, some would have visions, and some would dream things in dreams. I myself have had some wonderful dreams in the spirit, but I have not seen any visions with my sight, although I have seen visions in the spirit. However, visions and dreams, as well as casting out demons, are not listed among the nine aspects of the manifestation of the Holy Spirit as power upon us. This again proves that those nine are not all the aspects. Even if those nine were all the items of the manifestation of the Holy Spirit, speaking in tongues is only one of them. How then can we say that speaking in tongues is the necessary or even the initial evidence of the Spirit? This is too extreme.

SPEAKING IN TONGUES IN THE CASES IN ACTS

With regard to speaking in tongues, some may refer to the cases of the day of Pentecost, the house of Cornelius, and the twelve Ephesian believers. However, we need to read those passages with a proper discernment and logical understanding.

The One Hundred Twenty on the Day of Pentecost

Acts 2:4 is the strongest ground used by the Pentecostals who insist that everyone must speak in tongues. This verse says, "And they were all filled with the Holy Spirit and began to speak in different tongues, even as the Spirit gave to them to speak forth." Some say that this verse means that they all began to speak in tongues. However, we may use the same grammatical construction to say, "Last night at 7:30 we all came into the meeting and began to pray." This means that we all came into the meeting, but it does not mean that we all prayed. Verse 4 does not say, "They were all filled with the Holy Spirit in order to speak in tongues." It says they were all filled with the Holy Spirit *and* began to speak in tongues. To be filled with the Holy Spirit is one thing, but to speak in tongues is another. It is difficult to prove by verse 4 that all one hundred twenty disciples not only were filled with the Spirit but also spoke in tongues.

If we read this chapter logically and carefully, we can realize that not all the disciples spoke in tongues. If all one hundred twenty spoke in tongues, how could the people hear them clearly? Verses 9-11 refer to the dialects of less than twenty places. Some of those places may have contained more than one dialect, but the number of dialects was probably still under thirty. All one hundred twenty disciples were filled with the Holy Spirit, and many of them spoke in tongues, but probably not all did.

The Gentiles at the House of Cornelius

Concerning the house of Cornelius, Acts 10:44-46 says, "While Peter was still speaking these words, the Holy Spirit fell upon all those hearing the word. And the believers who were of the circumcision, as many as had accompanied Peter, were amazed, because on the Gentiles also the gift of the Holy Spirit had been poured out; for they heard them speaking in tongues and magnifying God." Verse 46 uses the conjunction *and.* This grammatical construction indicates that they did two things. They did not speak in tongues *to* magnify God; they spoke in tongues *and* magnified God. To speak in tongues is one thing, while to magnify God is another. When the people in the house of Cornelius received the Holy Spirit upon them, they did two things. One was to speak in tongues, and the other was to magnify God. We can be sure that they all were filled with the Holy Spirit, but we cannot be sure they all spoke in tongues. Perhaps some spoke in tongues while others magnified God.

The Ephesian Believers

Concerning the Ephesian believers, Acts 19:6 says, "And when Paul laid his hands on them, the Holy Spirit came upon them, and they spoke in tongues and prophesied." This sentence does not stop with "they spoke in tongues"; it says, "they spoke in tongues and prophesied." Should we believe that all twelve disciples did two things, both speak in tongues, on the one hand, and prophesy, on the other? This is not a logical understanding. The logical understanding is that after receiving the Holy Spirit upon them, some of the twelve spoke in tongues, and some of them prophesied. Not all that were present spoke in tongues. This also shows that speaking in tongues is not a necessity.

Those with a Pentecostal background insist that the cases in the above three passages—Acts 2, 10, and 19—prove that all believers who receive the baptism of the Holy Spirit must speak in tongues. However, if we use proper logic to understand and consider this matter, we cannot use these passages as proof. On the contrary, we can clearly see in 1 Corinthians 12 that not everyone speaks in tongues. Some speak in tongues as the evidence, or manifestation, of the Spirit, but others have a different manifestation. There is no guessing about this. Let us be clear according to the word of the Lord that speaking in tongues is but one of many items of the manifestation of the Holy Spirit as power upon us. It is not a necessary item, and it is not the initial item. Therefore, we should not oppose it, and we should not insist on it as a necessity.

THE WRONG TEACHING OF AN INITIAL EVIDENCE

In 1 Corinthians 12:30 Paul asks, "Do all speak in tongues?" We should not guess about the answer; rather, we should take the Word as it is. All do not speak in tongues. In 14:5 Paul says, "I desire that you all speak in tongues." This indicates that not all the Corinthians spoke in tongues. The Pentecostals say that all the early believers spoke in tongues, but if they did, there would have been no need for the apostle to say this.

Those who have a Pentecostal background insist that everyone who has the baptism of the Holy Spirit must speak in tongues. However, 1 Corinthians 12 is a problem to them, because it says that speaking in tongues is only one of many aspects of the manifestation of the Holy Spirit. Many of them reconcile this problem by saying that speaking in tongues as the initial and necessary evidence of the baptism of the Holy Spirit is one thing, but after that, to exercise the gift of speaking in tongues is another thing. After the initial evidence, they say, many lose the gift of tongues and perhaps only a few keep it.

An elderly brother, a leading missionary of the Assembly of God in the capital of China, told me that on the day of Pentecost when the Holy Spirit came down for the first time, all the disciples spoke with unknown tongues rather than human languages or dialects. Then when the people heard their voices and crowded around the disciples, the disciples began to speak actual dialects to them. This brother said that to experience the baptism of the Holy Spirit with the speaking of unknown tongues as the initial evidence is one thing, but after this to exercise the gift to speak in another language is another thing.

After he said this to me, I studied the Word intensely. I found that Acts 2:4 says that the disciples "began to speak in different tongues," while verse 6 says, "And when this sound occurred, the multitude came together and was confounded because each one heard them speaking in his own dialect." This indicates that before the people crowded to see the disciples, the disciples had been speaking in dialects, not unknown tongues. Verse 11 says, "We hear them speaking in our tongues the magnificent works of God." Even though the word used in this verse is *tongues,* not *dialects,* what they spoke was understandable.

After speaking in tongues when they receive the baptism of the Holy Spirit, nearly all the Pentecostal brothers and sisters continue to speak in tongues. Almost no one loses their speaking in tongues; once they speak in tongues the first time, they keep it. It is never the case that one thousand Pentecostals speak in tongues today, but after one week nine hundred fifty lose the gift and only fifty still speak in tongues. When they come together to meet, almost everyone speaks in tongues.

On the one hand, many of them say that not everyone exercises the gift of speaking in tongues, but on the other hand, they very much insist that everyone must speak in tongues. This is an awkward practice. There is no need to insist that speaking in tongues is the necessary and initial evidence of the baptism of the Holy Spirit. Speaking in tongues is simply one of many aspects of the manifestation of the Holy Spirit upon us as power. If today we have the power of the Holy Spirit upon us, we may heal someone, but if we do not have the power, we cannot heal anyone. Therefore, healing also is an aspect of the manifestation of the Holy Spirit. When many people receive the Holy Spirit as power upon them, they do not speak in tongues.

We must train our mind to consider these things in a very logical way. How can we speak of an "initial manifestation?" To cast out a demon by the power of the Holy Spirit today and to cast out another one next month is the same thing. We should not say that to cast out a demon is only our initial manifestation; later, we will continue to cast out demons.

Let us be clear, soberminded, logical, and sound in mind to understand the Word of God. Do not be perplexed or confused by the situation and the wrong teachings. Be sober in mind to read the Word and understand it carefully. Then we will see that healing, speaking in tongues, and casting out demons are just some of the many items of the manifestation of the Holy Spirit. There is no such thing as an "initial manifestation." This term is a human invention used to reconcile the wrong teaching that everyone must speak in tongues. This way of reconciling their teaching is unreasonable.

CARING ONLY FOR THE REAL
AND GENUINE EXPERIENCE OF THE SPIRIT

Many Pentecostals, although they insist that everyone must speak in tongues and that they themselves speak in tongues, doubt in their own heart whether they actually speak in tongues. They simply insist in this way because they

are on the Pentecostal line. This is the same as people under
certain kinds of government. They doubt that their government is right, but they insist that it is right simply because
they are under it. If we question some who speak in tongues
as to whether it is genuine, we will find that they doubt it.
They do not have the assurance that what they speak is real.
Rather, there are many imitations and much human manu-
facturing. We tried all these things. I myself spoke in
tongues, and I helped others to do it. I have seen real speaking in tongues, but not many tongues today are real.

Today the tongues movement has a wrong emphasis, and
it causes much damage. Therefore, we must spend time to dig
out these matters to clarify the situation, to help the believers
to be clear about this so that we may seek and gain the proper
experience.

I have studied these matters both in the Far East and in
the United States. Because the Pentecostal believers insist
that everyone must speak in tongues, they often force people
to do it. They preach this matter, they push it, and they even
teach people how to exercise their mouth to change their tone
to speak in unknown tongues. There is a strong influence
among them that forces everyone to do it.

The issue of this is that a number of them have been disappointed because they cannot do it. Even after trying to,
they still cannot receive this ability. Others have been forced
to imitate speaking in tongues. Some may be in the spirit but
not have speaking in tongues, so because they have the background of the Pentecostal teaching, they speak in tongues by
human imitation. I would like to speak freely with many Pentecostal believers. I wish to touch their conscience in a calm
way, asking, "Can you tell me in truth, with a good conscience,
that your speaking in tongues is the real and genuine
tongues?" When I asked some in this way, they replied, "We
cannot say whether or not it is genuine, but we feel it is help-
ful."

I have seen many human imitations and manufacturings.
In this country, some people teach others how to speak in
tongues by exercising their mouth to change their tone of
voice. While one such person was helping two Chinese

brothers in this way, his wife stood by and encouraged them, saying, "Do not speak in Chinese and do not speak in English. Just speak something else." This means that they were simply to change their tone of voice. As long as their speaking did not have the Chinese tone or the English tone, whatever came out would be speaking in tongues. One of the Chinese brothers eventually imitated a tone in a false way, and the husband and wife rejoiced. They wanted the brother to testify of his experience in the next meeting.

Some people have told me that when the Spirit works upon us, we must cooperate with Him by exercising our mouth. However, this is simply to cooperate by imitating. If the Holy Spirit does something miraculous with us, there is no need to exercise our mouth in this way. We can compare this to electricity. When electricity comes into an appliance, there is no need for the various parts of the appliance to "exercise to cooperate" in this way. To teach people to speak in tongues is not genuine. In 1960 some people came to me in this way. They laid hands on me and told me to say, "Praise Jesus" quickly over and over. This was supposed to be speaking in tongues.

At one point, I myself helped people to speak in tongues, but eventually I asked myself, "What is this? Before I had this kind of experience, I already loved the Lord and I experienced Him very much. Why do I have to do this?" After that time, I dropped this practice. In the many years since then, I have been helped by the Lord to know Him, to grow in Him, and to follow Him more and more deeply.

THE PURPOSE OF THE MANIFESTATION
OF THE HOLY SPIRIT

All the aspects of the manifestation of the Holy Spirit as power are for the purpose of life. The right, genuine speaking of tongues is to help people to grow in life. Many Pentecostals, however, do not know much of life. They speak in tongues for the purpose of speaking in tongues; they do not speak in tongues for life. On the day of Pentecost, the speaking in tongues was for the preaching of the gospel, and three thousand people were saved, but today many people speak in tongues for a display and a kind of entertainment. All the aspects of the Holy Spirit as power to us are for life. They are not life, but they are for life. Speaking in tongues in the right way is for the growth and edification in life. Even healing is for the growth in life. Today, however, many people misuse these matters because they know nothing about life.

I beg you to be soberminded and to have a clear and logical understanding of the Word. Is it logical to understand that speaking in tongues is a necessary requirement for the evidence, or manifestation, of the Holy Spirit? No, it is not logical. The logical way is to consider it as only one item of many aspects. We must be clear. I would ask you to read all the above passages again carefully and learn to study the Word carefully, clearly, and rightly. Do not be careless in studying and understanding the Word. Do not listen to the wrong teachings, such as how all twelve believers in Ephesus spoke in tongues. If we read portions of the Word such as Acts 19 in a careful way, we will find something different from these wrong teachings.

NOT BEING INFLUENCED BY OUR BACKGROUND, TEACHINGS, OR MENTALITY

Some have said that they cannot prove that their speaking in tongues is genuine and real. They themselves even doubt it. However, they say that when they speak in this way, they feel happy and they are helped. This is because as long as we have a heart to seek the Lord, He is always willing to meet us, and He is always gracious to us. Many Pentecostal believers have a heart to seek the Lord and to seek the Spirit, so the Lord meets them, not in the so-called Pentecostal way but in a general, spiritual way. Therefore, they feel very happy with the Lord. However, because they have the background of the Pentecostal teachings, influence, and mentality, they add the false speaking in tongues to their good experience of the Lord. This kind of speaking is not the genuine and real one. It is something they add on by exercising their mouth to change their tone of voice.

When I was in China, I spoke to many Pentecostal brothers about these things. I told them that we experience the

Lord just as they do. The difference between our experience and theirs, however, is that they have the Pentecostal mind and background, so when they have a good experience of the Lord, they add on speaking in tongues, although I doubt that their speaking in tongues is genuine. Because we do not have this kind of background, we experience the Lord without adding on anything.

I also asked certain ones who insist on speaking in tongues what the result of their work is, how many people they have won for the Lord, and whether the ones in their meetings are more spiritual than others. I was able to point out to them that there were one thousand brothers and sisters among us who have a good experience of the Lord; they are living, yet very few of them ever spoke in tongues. Those among us are never taught to speak in tongues, and they are never forced to do so. Because they do not have the idea, the mentality, or the background of this kind of teaching, when they have a good experience of the Lord, they do not add anything on.

Those among the Pentecostals, however, are often taught, forced, and influenced to speak in tongues. When they have a good experience with the Lord, they have the mentality, the idea, the background, and the teaching of tongues, so they simply exercise their mouth to change their tone and add something on. I doubt that what they add on is the real speaking in tongues.

This does not mean that I oppose the real speaking in tongues. I do not oppose it. I believe that even in these last days there is the real speaking in tongues. However, I doubt that what is added on by believers under the influence, force, and teaching of the Pentecostal movement is genuine.

BEING MODERATE, GENERAL, AND OPEN TO THE LORD

Recently, many people on the West Coast of the United States have been brought to the Lord by this kind of movement. However, in the Far East also many people were brought to the Lord by us, yet very few of them spoke in tongues. The great majority did not speak in tongues, but many were added to the Lord and are very much going on with the Lord. I do not like to criticize, but among those who have been brought to the Lord by the recent movements, I do not know how much real experience of the Lord they have. Rather, they are taught and influenced to add something on, which they say is speaking in tongues.

We are clear from the teaching of the Scriptures that speaking in tongues is but one of many items of the manifestation of the Holy Spirit upon us as power. If we spend time to objectively study the present situation, we will be clear that only a small portion of what is called speaking in tongues is real and genuine. The majority are human imitations and manufacturings. Therefore, we conclude that there is no need to insist that speaking in tongues is the necessary and initial evidence of the Spirit.

On the other hand, we should not oppose the real speaking in tongues. We must be very moderate, general, and open to the Lord. If the Lord gives us this gift, we simply receive it. If He does not give it to us, we just go along with Him. We leave this to the Lord, neither opposing it nor imposing it. We are open to Him.

Today we need the real experience of the Holy Spirit upon us as power. We should not be frightened away by the wrong teachings. We should not consider them. We simply must be clear that we need the Holy Spirit within us, and we also need the Holy Spirit upon us. We need to be filled with the Spirit as life within, and we need to be clothed and empowered with the Spirit as power outwardly.

In these days may we all go to the Lord to deal with Him about this, saying, "Lord, I do realize that I need this experience of the Holy Spirit as power to me." Then we should leave this open to the Lord. We should not regard speaking in tongues, and we should not oppose it. Leave it to the Lord, and have the real experience of the Holy Spirit as power. There are many aspects of the manifestation of the Spirit, of which speaking in tongues is only one. What we must experience is the Holy Spirit as power upon us.

CHAPTER FIVE

THE WAY TO EXPERIENCE THE INFILLING AND OUTPOURING OF THE SPIRIT

Scripture Reading: Acts 2:37-38, 33; Gal. 5:16-25; Acts 5:32

At this point we are clear that the work of the Holy Spirit is of two aspects: the outward aspect and the inward aspect. However, it is not sufficient only to know this. We should seek the experiences of the work of the Holy Spirit. The purpose of these lessons is to help our experience. I look to the Lord that those who receive these messages will have the intention, desire, and thirst to seek new and further experiences of the work of the Holy Spirit.

We need to experience the Holy Spirit in two aspects. We must experience the filling of the Holy Spirit within and the outpouring of the Holy Spirit upon us. On the one hand, we must renew our experience of being filled with the Holy Spirit, and on the other hand, we must seek the experience of the Holy Spirit being poured upon us. I am afraid that many brothers and sisters have never had the experience of the Holy Spirit being poured upon them. You need to begin to have this experience of the Holy Spirit's work; that is, you must experience the Holy Spirit upon you outwardly as power and release. Therefore, this message will contain little on the doctrinal side. Rather, it will address the practical way to experience the infilling and outpouring of the Holy Spirit, the work of the Spirit to fill us and to endue us.

THE WORK OF THE SPIRIT
BEING A GREAT PART OF THE GOSPEL

The work of the Holy Spirit is a great part of the gospel. We know the gospel, but we may not know it in a full way. Do we realize that the gospel includes the work of the Holy Spirit? Acts 2:37-38 says, "And when they heard this, they were pricked in their heart, and they said to Peter and the rest of the apostles, What should we do, brothers? And Peter said to them, Repent and each one of you be baptized upon the name of Jesus Christ for the forgiveness of your sins, and you will receive the gift of the Holy Spirit."

The way to receive the gospel of redemption and salvation is to repent, to believe in the Lord Jesus, and to be baptized in His name. This gospel includes two sides. The negative side is the remission, the forgiveness, of sins, and the positive side is the all-inclusive Holy Spirit as a gift to us. This includes the divine, eternal life; regeneration; the indwelling of the Holy Spirit; the outpouring, the baptism, of the Holy Spirit; and all the aspects of the work of the Holy Spirit. All the work of the Holy Spirit is included in the gospel, which we receive at the very moment we believe in the Lord Jesus.

As Christians we all believe that we have the remission of sins, but are we sure that we also have the gift of the Holy Spirit, including the baptism, the outpouring, of the Spirit? The proper way to answer this is to say that we have the gift of the Holy Spirit, but we have experienced and appropriated Him only to a certain extent. A friend may send us a large package of food, and we may receive it, but we may never open it and enjoy it. In the same way, we must recognize that the Holy Spirit already has been given to us. The Holy Spirit is a gift given to us based on the work of Christ for the remission of sins.

The Forgiveness of Sins
Being an Accomplished Fact

The remission of sins is based on the redemption of the Lord through His death on the cross. Without the shedding of blood, there is no possibility that God can forgive our sins, but the Lord shed His blood and died on the cross for our sins. This is an accomplished, finished work. Now we as sinners simply may come to Jesus to receive it.

When we preach the gospel, there is no need to tell sinners to ask God to forgive them. This is to preach in the wrong way. Rather, in our preaching we must tell people that Christ died on the cross. He has accomplished redemption, and remission of sins already has been given to us. Remission of sins is here already, waiting for us to receive it. Because we do not know the proper way to preach the gospel, we have not seen many people saved through our preaching. We should tell sinners not to ask God to forgive them, but to take what God already has given them.

We may illustrate this in the following way. I may have a nice Bible that I wish to give to a brother. The brother does not need to beg me for it. I am ready to give it to him, but he may still say, "Oh, please be good to me and give me a Bible." He may ask for it, but he may not take it. I may say to him, "What is the matter with you? Here is the Bible already." If the brother is wise, he will say nothing but "thank you" and take it. To preach the gospel is not to tell sinners to ask God to give them something. Rather, to preach the gospel is to tell sinners that God has given something to them already. Something is accomplished and ready. Something has been given to them and is here for them to take. If we know the proper way to preach the gospel, the Holy Spirit will honor this way and cause people to receive salvation.

The Holy Spirit Being a Gift Already Given to Us

It is the same with the gift of the Holy Spirit. The Holy Spirit is a gift that has already been given based on the work of Christ. After His crucifixion the Lord rose, and by His resurrection the Lord brought the Spirit of life to us. On the evening of the day of resurrection the Lord came to His disciples with the Spirit of life. He breathed into them and said, "Receive the Holy Spirit" (John 20:22). By His resurrection, Christ imparted the Spirit to us, and we were regenerated by the Spirit.

Following this, Christ ascended to the heavens, and by His ascension He poured down the Holy Spirit of power. In Acts 2:33 Peter said, "Therefore having been exalted to the right hand of God and having received the promise of the Holy Spirit from the Father, He has poured out this which you both see and hear." In order to preach the gospel, we must preach the Lord's death, the Lord's resurrection, and the Lord's ascension as the three steps of His work. By His crucifixion Christ bore our sins and redeemed us from sins; by His resurrection He imparted the Spirit of life into us; and by His ascension He poured down the Spirit of power upon His Body, including all of us as His members.

All this has been accomplished. Now we only need to realize these facts. If we are sinners, we must realize that Christ has died for our sins. Redemption has been accomplished, and all we have to do is receive it by saying, "Lord, I thank You. You have died for me." We realize the fact, and we take it to receive remission of sins. Following this, we realize that Christ has resurrected, and by His resurrection He has imparted life to us through the Spirit of life. All we must do is receive it, saying, "Lord, I praise You. You have resurrected, and You are the resurrection life." In this way, we receive the Spirit of life. Then in the same principle, we realize that the Lord has ascended and poured down the Holy Spirit. Now we simply receive by faith what the Lord has accomplished. May the Spirit open our eyes to see that He is ours already. There is no need to pray or ask for the Spirit. Rather, we simply acknowledge the fact and apply it.

I have read the histories and biographies of many people who had this kind of experience. Formerly, they had a certain knowledge, but they did not have a revelation. One day the revelation came to them, and they saw that the Holy Spirit was theirs already. Then they had a living faith, a claiming faith, and an applying faith, and they thanked the Lord. When they received this revelation and exercised living faith, they received their first experience of the Holy Spirit being poured upon them. Others have had a different experience. They saw the revelation and they received it, but it was only at a later time, not right away, that they experienced the power of the Holy Spirit. I have seen brothers and sisters in our meetings have this kind of experience, and many years ago I myself began to experience the power of the Holy Spirit. The most important thing is to see, to realize, that the gift of the all-inclusive Holy Spirit, not only the indwelling Spirit but also the outpoured Spirit, has been given and is ours already.

SENSING OUR NEED FOR THE OUTPOURED SPIRIT

We need to realize these facts, but we also must sense our need for them. We may realize that the Holy Spirit is ours, but do we need the Holy Spirit to be power to us? If we feel we do not need the Spirit, even if we have Him, we will not apply Him. We may have a large store of food, but if we are not hungry, we will not use it. Do we sense the need for the Holy Spirit as power? We must deal with our need, and we must deal with our indifference. We must not say that it does not matter whether or not we experience the Spirit in this way. Rather, we must have a positive attitude. We should say, "Lord, I must experience this. I am not satisfied with my present situation, with what I am today. I need something more." Then we can realize that the work of the Spirit has been accomplished, and the Spirit has been given. The entire, all-inclusive Holy Spirit is ours. However, only when we realize our need do we exercise our faith to apply the Spirit.

The first thing we must be clear about is that all things have been accomplished. Christ has died, resurrected, and ascended. Sins have been dealt with, and the Spirit has been given as life and poured down as power. We have repented, believed in the Lord, and have been baptized. Now all these things are ours. If we realize that all these are ours and we sense the need for them, we will apply them and enjoy them by faith. There is no need to pray that the Lord give us the Holy Spirit or pour Him out; He has been given and poured out already. All that remains is for us to realize what the Lord has accomplished, to realize that the Holy Spirit has been given, and to realize our need.

WALKING BY THE SPIRIT BY APPLYING THE CROSS

The way to experience the infilling of the Holy Spirit is in Galatians 5:16-25. The Spirit in this passage is the Spirit of life, who brings forth the fruit of life from within us. This portion of the Word tells us that we have this Spirit already; what we need is to walk by the Spirit. The way to walk by the Spirit is to realize the work of the cross. Verse 24 says, "But they who are of Christ Jesus have crucified the flesh with its passions and its lusts." We need to apply the work of the cross upon our flesh with its passions and lusts. The flesh here includes both the flesh and the soul. Passions and lusts are not only of the body. When a person dies, his body is still present, but the passions and lusts are gone. The passions and lusts of the fallen person are the desires of the soul, the soulish life, related to the body. This means that we must apply the cross to the soulish life.

The grammatical construction of verse 24 is very meaningful. It does not say in the passive voice that the flesh with its passions and lusts has been crucified. Rather, it says in the active voice that they who are of Christ Jesus have crucified it. This means that we apply the work of the Lord's cross upon our soulish life. It is notable, however, that the verb is in the perfect tense. We need to crucify the flesh, but we have done it already. This means that the crucifixion of the flesh has been accomplished by the Lord, but we now need to apply it.

Our flesh was crucified on the cross by the death of the Lord Jesus, but now we need to be active to apply to our soulish life what the Lord accomplished. If we do not apply the work of the cross, we will live in the soul. We will live under the direction of the passions and desires related to the flesh. Then there will be no room for the indwelling Spirit to fill us because we will be filled with something else. We need to be dealt with by the work of the cross so that we can give the ground, the room, to the Holy Spirit.

Verse 24 speaks of the cross, and verse 25 speaks of the Spirit, saying, "If we live by the Spirit, let us also walk by the Spirit." To apply the work of the cross to the soulish life, the natural life, with its passions and desires related to the body is the only way to walk by the Spirit. The more we apply the cross to our soulish life, our self, our natural life, the more we will walk by the Spirit, and the more the Spirit will fill us. The only way to be filled with the Holy Spirit is to apply the work of the cross to our natural life.

We need to take some time to go to the Lord to deal with Him and to let Him deal with us. We must ask Him to reveal to us the passions, desires, and other things of the soulish life we need to deal with. This is not a once-for-all matter. We always need to deal in this way. Day by day, even moment by moment, we need to apply the cross of the Lord to our soulish life with its passions and desires related to this sinful body. This is the only way to walk by the Spirit.

We have the Spirit, but we need to apply the Spirit, and the only way to apply the Spirit of life within us and let Him fill us is to apply the cross to our soulish life. There is no other way. Therefore, we need to spend more time with the Lord, not praying that He do this or that for us as matters of business, but that He would bring us into His light. We need to do this in the morning and in the evening, day by day. We should forget about our matters of business. Even if we are sick, we should forget about our sickness. We have a spiritual illness that is more serious. We must simply go to the Lord, and not only once. We need real experiences of these matters.

Until 1931, six years after I was saved, I was with a group of believers who studied the Word but were spiritually dead in their study. Day by day, every morning, I went to the Lord. In those times, I did not have any prayer about matters of business. For about six months the only thing I prayed day by day was, "Lord, bring me into Your light and show me where I am and what is within me." It was wonderful. Day by day the Lord showed me something natural, worldly, sinful, soulish, or fleshly within me that I needed to deal with. That was the application of the cross in prayer by the power of the Holy Spirit. Every morning I experienced the infilling of the Holy Spirit. Every morning after I prayed, I was full of joy. In those days I dared not to sing a certain hymn about how the name of the Lord Jesus is like music, because whenever I sang it, my tears came down. I constantly sensed the filling of the Holy Spirit.

To be sure, if at that time I had had the teachings and background of the Pentecostal movement, I would have added speaking in tongues to my experience. Eventually, in 1936, I did add speaking in tongues, but in 1931 I did not have this kind of teaching. I simply experienced the Lord to a full extent without any kind of strange speaking.

The only way to experience the infilling of the Holy Spirit

is to be dealt with by the cross in the light of the Holy Spirit. If we try to keep something for ourselves, we are finished. We must deal with all the soulish, natural, worldly, and sinful things within us, applying the work of the cross to them in the power of the Holy Spirit. Then we can constantly walk by the Spirit and have the experiences of the Spirit.

THE WAY TO EXPERIENCE THE OUTPOURING OF THE HOLY SPIRIT

Apparently, the outpouring of the Holy Spirit is hard to experience, but in actuality it is very easy. It depends on several things. First, it depends on our need. Do we truly sense the need for the outpouring of the Spirit, or are we just talking about it? Many Christians today do not sense the need of the Holy Spirit upon them as power. We should ask the Lord to cause us to sense the need. We have the Spirit already, but we need to apply the Spirit and experience Him. If we do not have the need, there is no need to talk about this.

Second, we need a special, specific consecration. If we sense the need, we must consecrate ourselves again to experience the Holy Spirit as power upon us.

Third, we must be obedient. Acts 5:32 says that God gives the Holy Spirit to those who obey Him. If we never deal with the Lord, we will not know how disobedient we are. In the previous century, a certain sister sought the baptism of the Holy Spirit. Seeking this experience, she prayed and consecrated herself to the Lord. Women at that time had long hair, which they wore high on their head. When this sister prayed, she sensed that the Lord was demanding that she "tear down the tower" on her head by cutting her hair. However, she would not obey. One night when meeting with some Christians, she prayed, "Lord give me the experience," but the Lord said, "Give me your hair." Eventually she made the decision to obey the Lord and cut her hair, and at that very moment she experienced the baptism of the Holy Spirit.

I met another sister who lived outside of Beijing, the ancient capital of China. She came from country people who lived on farms. Before she was saved, a large chicken belonging to her neighbor wandered on to her farm, and she caught it and killed it. When the neighbor came to find the chicken, she lied and said that she did not know where it was. After a few years she was saved, and in the church there was much prayer for the experience of the power of the Holy Spirit. She also was one seeking this experience. For many days whenever she knelt down to pray to the Lord for the power of the Holy Spirit, her prayer had no answer. Rather, the thought of a large chicken came to her mind. One day she remembered how she had taken her neighbor's chicken. She bought a chicken larger than the first one, took it to the neighbor, and confessed. Immediately after that she received the experience of the baptism of the Holy Spirit.

There are many stories such as these. Some persons could not experience the power of the Holy Spirit simply due to one sin. This shows us how we must be obedient. If we sense the need for the Spirit and we consecrate ourselves to the Lord, we must be obedient.

Fourth, if there is no struggle between us and the Lord, we may simply receive the experience of the Spirit by claiming it. We should not care about our feelings; we should just receive by claiming.

I have had many personal experiences of this kind. I know that to serve the Lord I need power, so I sense the desperate need of the Spirit. Second, I consecrate myself to the Lord. Third, I fear only one thing, that is, a struggle between me and the Lord. Struggling with the Lord is awful. To have a struggle with the Lord is serious. There have been many false rumors about me, but by the grace of the Lord I am not afraid of them. The only thing I am afraid of is a struggle between me and the Lord. As long as there is no struggle between me and the Lord, I am afraid of nothing. If there is a struggling between you and the Lord, I beg you to deal with it right away. Then you can receive the experience of the Spirit by claiming it.

A TESTIMONY OF THE EXPERIENCE
OF THE POWER OF THE HOLY SPIRIT

I can personally testify of the experience of the outpouring of the Spirit. Once when I began to minister, I had no particular feeling. However, after I began to minister, I had the sense that a cloud came down upon me to encompass, encircle, and cover me. At that point my ministering changed very much. To have that kind of realization was a unique experience in my whole life. To be sure, that was not my imagination; it was something real.

In another church meeting, I ministered the message in an ordinary way without any special feeling. The next day, however, a brother told me that his high-school-age son saw a man standing by me in a very brilliant robe while I was ministering, making the same gestures I made. This went on for twenty minutes, after which the man left. This was an experience of the liberty, anointing, release, power, and even authority of the Word. This happened more than once.

On another occasion, a brother came into the Lord's Day meeting after my ministering had begun. When he looked at the platform, he was very surprised, wondering how many persons were there. He saw clearly that while I was ministering, another person was standing by me for a long time. This was not a dream, his light talk, or a joke. The brother who saw this was a soberminded brother over fifty years old. Several times people have told me that they saw the same thing. On one occasion, a brother told me that on the Lord's Day before my ministering began, as I was praying on the platform, he saw three persons there, me and two other persons with me.

I do not wish to attract you to pay attention to this kind of experience. Rather, I must testify to you that there is no need to have a feeling. We simply must deal with the Lord in the right way and stand on the right position, saying, "Lord, I am redeemed by You and now I am Yours. There is nothing between You and me, so I have the right, the position, to claim what is mine." This is sufficient. We simply realize our need, and claim and take it. Then the Lord will make it real. There is no need for us to feel or sense anything. According to my experiences, the Lord sometimes grants us to sense something, such as the cloud that came down upon me. However, many times I did not feel anything. I simply had the release, the freedom, the liberty, to minister. It seemed very ordinary to me, but something special was there. There are many different ways the Holy Spirit comes to work with us if we are in the right position.

I cannot exhaust all the stories of what I have experienced while preaching the gospel from the platform. In my preaching of the living word there was something of the power of the Holy Spirit. Once when we preached the gospel, I gave a call to the audience, asking them to respond by standing up. I gave them a hymn to sing and told them that anyone who was moved by the Holy Spirit should stand during the singing of the hymn. Our main hall was filled with people, so we had opened another room. Many people in the main hall stood up, but no one in the second room stood, although there were many people there. Suddenly I had the feeling to speak something. I turned in a certain direction and said, "There is someone like a devil keeping people from standing up." After I said this, many people stood up, beginning with a mother and her daughter. Later I found out that when I spoke that word about a devil, that daughter was struggling to keep her mother from standing up. The mother wished to stand, but the daughter struggled to keep her sitting down. While they were struggling, I turned in their direction and said, "There is someone like a devil keeping people from standing up." That daughter became frightened and began to tremble. Then the mother stood up, followed by the daughter, and all the rest of the people. To be sure, this was something of the power of the Holy Spirit.

Do not pay attention to the manifestation or the feelings. We should forget about them. Rather, we must realize that the Holy Spirit is a gift given to us. He is ours; He is our portion already. Then we must realize our need, consecrate ourselves, be obedient, and deal with the Lord until there is no struggle between us and the Lord. Then we simply receive. The Spirit is ours, and whenever there is a need, we receive Him. Then we will see how prevailing and powerful we will be. Many times we will not have the conscious sense, but we will have the Spirit. This is the right way. In these days we need to see the infilling and the outpouring of the Holy Spirit.

I can give many more stories from my experience, such as stories of dreams under the power and moving of the Holy

Spirit. However, we should forget about the manifestation and the feeling. We leave this matter to the Lord. We simply must deal with the above matters in a proper way. Day by day we apply the work of the cross to our natural life with the passions and desires related to the flesh. We also always realize that we need the Holy Spirit as power, so we consecrate ourselves to the Lord and deal with Him until there is no struggle between us and Him. Then we receive the Holy Spirit. He is ours.

Chapter Six

THE MINGLING OF THE OUTWARD AND INWARD WORK OF THE SPIRIT

Scripture Reading: 1 Cor. 12:28-30; 14:39

The experiences of the Holy Spirit as life within and as power without are different aspects of our experience, but they are the work of the same one Spirit, not two Spirits. According to the New Testament, the one Spirit works upon us, with us, and in us in different steps. In the first step, the Holy Spirit comes in to regenerate us, and as the last step, the Holy Spirit comes upon us to be power. We need to experience the Spirit in all these steps.

The Holy Spirit within us is the Lord, the living Person who directs us, and the Holy Spirit upon us is the power that we direct by the inner life. On the one hand, the Spirit is the Lord Himself to be life to us within, and since He is our Lord, we need to honor and obey Him. On the other hand, the Lord Himself is the Spirit as power upon us to be applied and directed by us. The Holy Spirit within us as life requires that we follow Him, but the Holy Spirit upon us always follows us as the power under our direction. As a result, the Lord is in us, we are in the Lord, and we and the Lord are mingled together. On one side, we obey the Lord and honor Him as the Lord, while on the other side, the Lord is under our direction for us to apply as power. This is the full, complete work and experience of the Holy Spirit.

REALIZING OUR NEED
OF LIFE WITHIN AND POWER WITHOUT

We must experience this Spirit up to the last step. We may not feel that we need to experience the Holy Spirit as power, but day by day we do need this experience. To come to the prayer meeting, the fellowship meeting, and the Lord's table meeting, we need power. Many times the brothers and sisters come to the meetings in a quiet way. They do not have the release, the liberty, or the power. They may think that when they attend the meetings, they do not need power; they can simply go to sit, look, listen, and say "amen." Some have told me that the meeting is a happy, restful time for them. After working all day, the meeting is a good time for rest. For them, to sit and listen to a nice message or some nice prayers is like enjoying music. However, even when we come just to enjoy the meetings, we still need power. If we come to the meetings with power, we will be released; we will have release and liberty.

As a brother who ministers the word to others, I need the listeners to have power; then I can minister in a better way. The more you are powerful, the more I am powerful. We may illustrate this by considering what would happen if there were only chairs, not people, in the room. If I came to minister to a room full of lifeless chairs, I could not minister for more than five minutes; because the chairs are lifeless, I will be lifeless. The more the listeners are living and powerful, the more the minister is living and powerful. There is a living response and reaction within him. If we come even to a message meeting with power, we will be a great help to the meeting. We will release the meeting.

To have power is to be released. If we have power, we are released from darkness, from the evil force, which is the kingdom of Satan. Many times when some brothers and sisters come to the meetings, a part of the kingdom of Satan in darkness is there; the evil force comes in with them, causing a battle. If each one, however, comes into the meeting with power, there is a great release. To come to the meeting, we need power. We should come in power because we are coming to serve the Lord. We must not think that the meeting is the business, the job, of the ministering brother. Rather, we all must come in power.

There is a difference between life and power. Life is for us, ourselves, but in order to minister life to others, we need power. Even to contact one another and fellowship in our daily life, we need power. Without power, we may have life, but we cannot minister what we have to others. Power transmits what we have as life to others. Then when others receive it, the power becomes life in them. When we preach the gospel in power, for example, the audience is moved by this power, and when they receive the gospel, the power becomes life within them. The power and life are of the same Spirit. Power is not life, but power is for life.

Even though we have the Holy Spirit, we may not apply the power because we do not realize our need for it. However, even to render a thanks to the Lord for a meal requires power. We may think that it is a small thing to return thanks to the Lord. We may simply say, "Thank You for the food. You are so good to us." However, we may not sense the need for power to give thanks. If we sense our need for power, we will realize our need for it even in small matters. Then we will deal with the Lord.

We need power to contact others, to fellowship with the saints, to come to the meetings, to listen to a message, to pray, and to praise the Lord. We should not think that only the apostles such as Peter and Paul need power. Rather, every Christian needs power. Day by day we need life within and power without. Even when we pray in our room, we need power to pray, and when we read a book, we need power to read. If we realize our need of life within and power without, day by day and moment by moment, we will claim it and apply it.

The outward aspect and the inward aspect eventually meet and mix together. The inward aspect is like a reservoir of water, while the outward aspect is like the rain. The rain and the reservoir join together until we cannot tell which is which. Both are the same water. We have the inward bubbling reservoir and the outward rain. This is the normal Christian life. If someone has only the outward rain, after a certain time there will be nothing left. We need to have the full experience of the indwelling of the Spirit and the full experience of the outpouring of the Spirit. Day by day we must be persons filled with the Spirit within and clothed with the Spirit without, persons in the Holy Spirit and with the Holy Spirit in us. This is the one Holy Spirit within and without, for life and for power. This is the proper issue of our experience.

COMING TO THE MEETINGS WITH LIFE AND POWER

Let us pray that we all will be brought to the point that we have the infilling and the outpouring. Then whenever we come together, there will be something powerful upon us and through us toward others. This is the proper position, condition, situation, and issue. May we pray in this way that we may be enabled to realize how much we need the Holy Spirit within and without, for life and for power. If we pray in this way, whenever we come together, our meeting will be changed much. We will honor the Holy Spirit, and the Holy Spirit will be with us. When we come together, we will be full of the Holy Spirit within us, among us, upon us, and outside of us, and in whatever we do there will be the presence of the Holy Spirit. Even if we have a little talk after the meeting, we will be full of the Holy Spirit. The outsiders will sense that there is something different with us. The real Bethel of Jacob's dream in Genesis 28:12-19 will be fulfilled in us. Heaven will be opened, and this place will be the very place of God's dwelling. People will sense the presence of the Lord, and this will be the real place for the stones to be poured upon with oil, that is, with the Holy Spirit.

We should not say that we do not need power. In all Christian matters we need life and we need power. Therefore, we must go to the Lord to pray and deal with this matter. Certain ones should not read too much. They should close their books and use more time to pray for the experience of the infilling and outpouring of the Holy Spirit. Then when they come to the meeting, they will be very different. Their prayer will not be dry; it will be full of the living water and full of the oil. By listening to our prayers, people can realize to what extent we experience the Holy Spirit.

I do not look down on knowledge; rather, I respect and value knowledge. However, all our knowledge must be in the Holy Spirit. If it is not in the Spirit, it is merely knowledge in letter with no reality. I respect the proper knowledge, but I do not care for so-called theology with every kind of "ism." Let us forget about the "isms." We need to exercise our spirit to pray more to experience the Spirit. Then we will be living and powerful whenever we come together.

Many people have told me that when they come to the meetings they are very impressed, not by the teaching or doctrine, but by the living atmosphere, the living water, and the oil, the anointing. However, I am still not satisfied with our Lord's Day meeting. Many come to this meeting in a loose way. They should not think that they have no responsibility for the meeting. They have responsibility simply because they come to the meeting. If the brothers and sisters come to the meeting with power, even before the ministry starts, there will be the moving, the current, the flowing of the Holy Spirit in the meeting place.

A TESTIMONY OF THE WORK OF THE SPIRIT

Between 1941 and 1943 in north China, every time the brothers and sisters came together, even before the meeting started we could already sense the Spirit. In 1943 we had a continual meeting for one hundred and eight days, day by day. It was wonderful. When people came into the meeting, they would begin to weep. No one would talk lightly. Instead many would sit there and weep without speaking. Eventually the unbelievers realized that if they came to our meeting place, they could not resist the Spirit. When they came in, they fell down, not physically but psychologically and spiritually. They were subdued by the living power. Some people even were saved by walking past the meeting place. A certain unbelieving school teacher rode a bicycle past the meeting place and noticed a verse painted in large characters on the wall. He was very moved by it, and he stopped, took off his hat, and prayed a short prayer, saying, "God, I am a sinner. Save me. I believe Jesus is my Lord and Savior." After a few weeks, he came to be baptized and told us his story.

A number of others were saved through dreams. One man was the husband of a sister, a deaconess, in the church. He came to a gospel meeting, and he and his friend were saved. The night before this friend came to the gospel meeting, he had had a dream. Then when he came to the meeting, he saw the meeting hall and said, "Last night I saw this in a dream. What I saw was exactly the same as this." On that day at that very moment, he repented with tears and was saved. This happened due to one reason: Most of the believers among us at that time were very much under the power of the Holy Spirit.

In that meeting place there were many rooms, but there was no noise. Instead, everyone was praying much in groups of three or five in each room. There were not many voices; the saints were silent but were praying all the time. During the preaching of the gospel, some would kneel and pray until the message was over. After that, they came out to take care of the after-meeting work.

I cannot relate how wonderful this situation was. However, I did not observe that even one person spoke in tongues. We do not oppose speaking in tongues; rather, we are open to it. Yet there was none at that time, but the situation was very prevailing and powerful. By this we should realize that we do need the power of the Holy Spirit. If we all experience the power, our coming together day by day will be different. It will be another kind of situation. The release, the liberty, the power, the presence of the Lord, the living water, and the oil will always be ministered to others, and there will be a living flow in the meeting.

In those years in China, whenever we came together, we sensed something flowing and moving. At that time, no one could resist the Lord's table meeting. Whoever came was melted by that meeting. I cannot relate how wonderful the presence and anointing of the Lord was.

Once during the one hundred and eight days, I gave a prayer before I ministered. I could not stop praying. I prayed for more than a half hour. The words came out like a waterfall. At a certain point, I lifted up my hands, although I did not notice it. A brother who was taller than I came to the platform to help support my arms. Later, people told me that the whole congregation also lifted up their hands. That was a unique and wonderful time. The words and sentences of that prayer shook the heavens, shook the earth, shook the hearts, and shook the families. We witnessed that nearly everyone was filled with shaking. The shaking and prayer went on for more than half an hour with no repetitions but with different sentences and utterances. This was a marvelous manifestation of the Holy Spirit.

This is the kind of Christian meeting we should have. I expect that one day our general Lord's Day meeting will be like this. Therefore, we need power to come to the meetings. What happened in China was the ultimate issue of the work of the Spirit, the outward working of the Spirit mingled and mixed together with the inward working. This was the complete, full work and experience of the one Holy Spirit.

TAKING THE PROPER, MODERATE, AND GENERAL WAY

What I have spoken in these messages is the compilation of many good teachings of the past, including those of the Brethren, the mystics such as Madame Guyon and Father Fenelon, and the inner life teachers such as Mr. Stockmayer, F. B. Meyer, Andrew Murray, and Mrs. Penn-Lewis. We have also received from others' experiences and even from the Pentecostal movement, and we have had our own experiences. I have studied the subject of the work of the Holy Spirit for more than thirty years, and I have the full assurance that our attitude is the moderate and right one.

In Christianity there are two groups of people with regard to the work of the Holy Spirit. One is the fundamental people with the Brethren teaching. They say that all the supernatural gifts and miraculous things are over and that there is no more divine healing or speaking in tongues. After studying this for thirty years, we conclude that we cannot go along with this teaching. It is too extreme. We have studied the Word carefully for this purpose, and we cannot find even a hint to support this teaching. No one can point out a verse to prove it. Rather, we found out that among the Brethren there was much divine healing. They themselves received such experiences, but they used different terms to describe it. They said it is not the healing of gifts but the healing of grace. This is simply a matter of terminology. If we call a man a dog, a cat, or a fish, he is still a man. In the same way, whether the

Brethren call what they experienced divine healing or something else, it is still some kind of divine healing.

On the other hand, there is the Pentecostal movement, especially the movement for the speaking in tongues. I am bothered about this movement. It also is too extreme. We do not agree that speaking in tongues is over. Who can tell us it is over? It is still here. However, people in the tongues movement insist that everyone has to speak in tongues. I recently read in a magazine that came out of that movement that those people realize that tongues is only one gift out of many. In 1 Corinthians 12:28, the apostle Paul said, "And God has placed some in the church: first apostles, second prophets, third teachers; then works of power, then gifts of healing, helps, administrations, various kinds of tongues." In this list, tongues is the last item.

Verses 29-30 continue, "Are all apostles? Are all prophets? Are all teachers? Do all have works of power? Do all have gifts of healing? Do all speak in tongues? Do all interpret tongues?" However, although certain persons have realized that there is such a word in the Scriptures, they still insist that everyone must speak in tongues. They have found a way to reconcile their teaching with the Scriptures. They say that in the church gatherings, not all the believers have the anointing to speak in tongues. Only a few have the anointing. That is why Paul indicated that not all speak in tongues. However, they say that every believer in his or her private devotional time must have the anointing to speak in tongues.

How can it be that in a private time everyone must have the anointing to speak in tongues, but in the gathering of the church it is possible for only a few to have the anointing to speak in tongues? This is not logical. Verse 29 asks, "Are all apostles?" We cannot say that some are apostles only when the church comes together, but outside of the church gatherings they are not apostles. If some are apostles in the meetings, they are also apostles outside the meetings. In their private devotional hour they are apostles, and in the hour of meeting they are still apostles. In the same way, if one has the anointing, the gift, to speak in tongues in the private hour, to be sure he will have it in the meetings. Likewise, if he has it in the meetings, he will have it in the private hour. It is not logical to say that everyone must speak in tongues in their private devotional hour, but only a few have the anointing to speak in tongues in the meeting. Some say this simply to insist that everyone must speak in tongues. This is too extreme. My intention is not to oppose speaking in tongues. It is simply to help you not to be extreme.

To say that we must speak in tongues creates trouble and causes many to be disappointed because they cannot obtain this gift. It also gives rise to many human imitations. The magazine I read insists that everyone must speak in tongues, but it admits that everyone who speaks in tongues doubts that what they speak is genuine and real. The reason people who speak in tongues doubt their experience is that the tongues movement influences people to imitate tongues by using a different kind of voice.

After people are influenced to speak in this way, they doubt that what they have done is real. I had the same experience in 1933, but a few years later I dropped it. After speaking in tongues in a miraculous and supernatural way on the day of Pentecost, did the disciples doubt their speaking? They did not doubt it, because what they had was the real item. The reason a person doubts his speaking is that it seems even to him that it is not miraculous or supernatural. He simply opens his mouth and uses his tongue to speak something. Then he doubts whether it comes from the Holy Spirit.

Although many people in that movement say that they speak in tongues, the tongue they speak in is something doubtful even to themselves. Every person who speaks in tongues has this experience. I do not oppose anyone, but I must be faithful to the Lord and to His children. I wish to help you to be released. Do not be frightened away from seeking the real experience of the power of the Holy Spirit, but do not be troubled to think that you must speak in tongues. There is no such need.

Not all speak in tongues, just as not all are apostles or prophets and not all have the gift of healing. We must leave this matter open to the Lord in a general way. We should not oppose it or insist on it and push it. If the Lord gives us this gift, we receive it with thanks, but we do not insist on it. Then we will be open and general, and we will not go to this extreme or the other extreme. We do not say that all miraculous and supernatural things are over, and neither do we say that everyone must speak in tongues, forcing and influencing people to imitate and do something false.

In 1 Corinthians 14:39 Paul says, "Do not forbid the speaking in tongues." Therefore, in chapters twelve and fourteen he indicates both that not all speak in tongues and that we should not forbid speaking in tongues. We must be general and open in a proper way. I say once again, forget about the manifestation. Leave this matter to the Lord. Perhaps He will give us to speak in tongues. If so, we should be thankful and receive it, but if He would give us other aspects of the manifestation of the Spirit, we receive those. We leave this to Him. The most important thing is that we experience life within and power without.

SPEAKING IN TONGUES
NOT BEING A PROOF OF POWER

Some may say that even if speaking in tongues is not real, it helps people to seek the Lord. Still, it is not necessary. I have seen a church of one thousand people experience the Lord in a good way, even better than those in the tongues movement, but we never insisted that they speak in tongues. Perhaps only one or two out of one hundred had the real experience from the Lord of speaking in tongues. I also have had good experiences of the Lord, especially in those years in China, but I did not speak in tongues at that time.

I reasoned in this way with a brother who was very much for speaking in tongues. In his district many people were saved, but in another district many more people were saved who did not speak in tongues, and they became more spiritual than the ones who did. They even opposed speaking in tongues, but they were more prevailing than the others. This proves that the power is not in the speaking in tongues. Some had speaking in tongues but not the power, while others did not have the speaking in tongues, but they had power. In this case, the speaking in tongues that the first group had is questionable.

As a rule, it is doubtful that speaking in tongues is a proof that one has power. If someone speaks in tongues but does not have power, he should doubt his tongues. What kind of speaking in tongues is this? If one has the genuine speaking in tongues, it must bring him power. There is no need to oppose anything, but we must help others. Do not be bothered by the wrong teaching to be forced to imitate something. This is too extreme. Let us be moderate, general, and open.

We need the real experience of the Holy Spirit within as our life and without as our power. We must seek this with a sincere heart and pray more that we will experience the Holy Spirit more in the proper way.